More stage dialects.

FT. CROCKETT

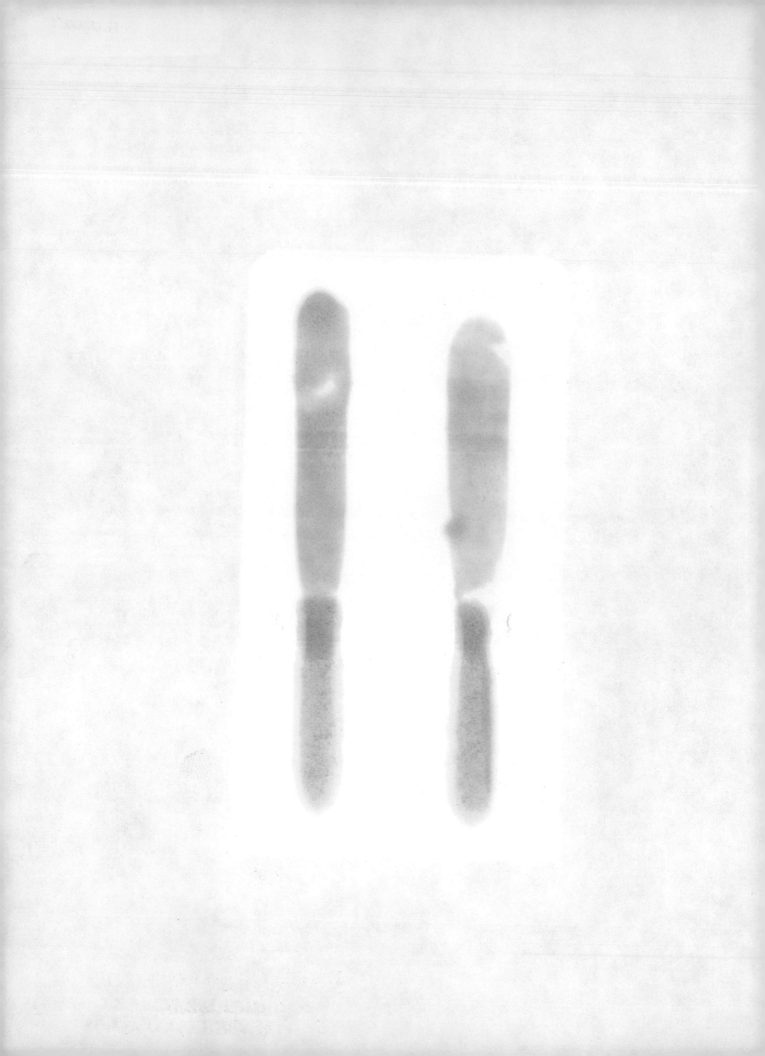

More Stage Dialects

More Stage Dialects

Jerry Blunt

1817

HARPER & ROW, PUBLISHERS, New York

Cambridge, Hagerstown, Philadelphia, San Francisco,
London, Mexico City, São Paulo, Sydney

Sponsoring Editor: Alan M. Spiegel
Project Editor: Brigitte Pelner
Production Manager: Jeanie Berke
Compositor: Bi-Comp, Incorporated
Printer and Binder: The Murray Printing Company
Art Studio: J&R Technical Services, Inc.

More Stage Dialects

Library of Congress Cataloging in Publication Data
Main entry under title:
  More stage dialects.

    Includes index.
    1. Acting. 2. English language—Pronunciation by
foreigners. I. Blunt, Jerry.
PN2071.F6M6   427   79-20873
ISBN 0-06-040784-0

To the donors
all around the world
whose voices, reproduced on the tapes, are the
basis for this book

Contents

༺ᨆᨆᨆᨆᨆᨆᨆᨆᨆᨆᨆᨆᨆᨆᨆᨆᨆᨆᨆᨆᨆᨆᨆᨆ༻

Preface

To one who has lived long enough to see the dramatic growth of new nation-states and to note their impact upon older more established societies, the time taken to shift an individual's, or a country's, interest from purely local matters to international concerns is amazingly short indeed.

This is a matter of importance to all in the theatre who are concerned with the creative process. As surely as the playwright, director, and actor of a century ago dealt with the local problem of a mortgage on the old homestead, and those same professional people in pre-World War II times broadened their outlook to cover the themes of such plays as *Street Scene*, *Mourning Becomes Electra*, *Winterset*, and *You Can't Take it with You*, today's theatre activists must spread their attention to matters that are world wide in scope.

The problems of the peoples of every continent impinge upon the problems of those of us in this country. Each day the news media reassert this fact. These problems, with their surrounding conditions, are the subject materials of our drama. It is no accident, then, that the contents of this book—three decades of collections—originally intended solely as backup reference sources for the author, his students, and the professional members of his community, are now offered to meet the needs of the playwright, director, and actor who must deal with subject materials, in plays and on film, that involve the problems of the people of Europe (West and East), Asia, the Near East, Africa, South America, and our own continent.

The speech of these people, valid in pronunciation, rhythm, and altered word order, is ready here in this volume—in print and on tape—for the use of those who desire an encyclopedic reference for present or future needs.

ACKNOWLEDGMENTS

For help freely and fully given, it is gratifying to express my thanks, first of all to the donors and then to the following people: Betty Andrews, Roscoe Lee Browne, Carolee Campbell, Professor Arnold Colbath, Don Davies, Ann Distler, Dr. Antonie Distler, Shay Duffin, Hector Elizondo, Nik and Lisa Karelis, Terence Kilburn, Dr. Lee Korf, Professor Charles Lewis, Dr. James Luter, David McMurty, Jim Mathews, Myra W. Menard, Professor Sanford Robbins, Stavros Romanos, James Ware, and Henry Zakohevsky.

Introduction

More Stage Dialects is designed as a companion to *Stage Dialects*.[1] Each complements the other. *Stage Dialects* is an in-depth study of limited range. *More Stage Dialects* is just the opposite; it is global in scope and almost unlimited in coverage. The purpose of *Stage Dialects*, a text with tapes, is to provide the actor, director, or playwright with an organized lesson plan—explanations, vocal drills, and practice paragraphs—for each subject. In contrast, *More Stage Dialects*, also a text with tapes, presents the user with the unorganized raw materials from which a dialect or an accent can be made and mastered.

Stage Dialects concentrates on the 11 dialects most used in the American theatre. The number was obtained by reviewing the plays listed over the last 50 years in our American play catalogues. These 11 dialects are New York/Brooklynese, American Southern, Standard English, Cockney, Irish, Scots, French, Italian, German, Russian, and Japanese.[2]

In complement, *More Stage Dialects* avoids duplication of the subjects in *Stage Dialects* and offers the student 56 dialects as heard in the voices of 88 individuals from 37 countries. The recordings of these voices were obtained over long periods of time and by means of extensive travel.[3]

A Library of Dialects

The process of obtaining the recordings of the dialects began 35 years ago during World War II when as Academic Head of the Chinese Training Program in the Air Force I tackled the problem of communication between Chinese pilots and crews and our own service personnel. Then, as now, a tape recorder was used—a very simple and limited instrument indeed. Called a mirrorphone, it could record only one minute of speech. A short spool of wire, after being rewound, gave a fairly clear reproduction of the recorded sound. Thus began also my first study of a Chinese accent. Since that time, fortunately, new instrumentation has allowed the making and keeping of what is now an extensive library of native dialects and foreign accents.

DEFINITION

"A *dialect* is a distinctive form of pronunciation, language structure, and vocabulary which is identified with a geographical area or a social

---

[1] Jerry Blunt, *Stage Dialects* (New York: Harper & Row, 1967).

[2] Japanese is an exception to the most used category. There has been, to be sure, a limited demand for it. However, its requirements of manipulative skills and the enjoyment of its sounds—"rots of ruck"—urged its inclusion in preference to Swedish, say, or Chicano, for which there has been a limited demand.

[3] A few (7 or 8) were taped in my home or office.

1

class. In varying degrees it possesses notable melodic and rhythmic patterns. It develops its own idiom. Further, a dialect is created whenever anyone speaks in a language not his own. Although such speech is often referred to as a foreign accent, it is one more form of dialectal expression. . . .

"If a dialect is nothing else, it is distinctive. Pronunciation and a peculiar use of idiom set one type of speech apart from another. The resultant contrast acts to sharpen an auditor's awareness of the special qualities each possesses. The difference is attractive—one of the reasons why a dialect compels attention as ordinary speech does not. It is no wonder that playwrights and actors, aware of this attractiveness, continually make use of it.

"Even as a dialect attracts, it instructs. The sounds of a dialect inform the ear in much the same way that a costume instructs the eye. *Where*, and, in part, *who*, are revealed by dialect. The place where a person is, or comes from, and his socio-economic standing can simply and concisely be told by his form of speech. A dialect, then, is an expressive tool."[4]

Dialectal Elements

It may be assumed that all speech in every language is uttered as a dialect of one sort or another. For example, although we do not refer to it as such, what we now call Standard American speech, that is, the syllabification and word order now habitual in the speech of most Americans, is, in fact, a dialect in itself. However, common usage usually denotes as dialects only those particular speech forms that vary from the largest standardized group. Hence, we speak of a Midwestern, a Yorkshire, or an Australian dialect, even though in the latter case Australia is a nation and a continent in itself and is located on a separate island all its own but does vary from a parental speech called Standard English.

A dialect can gain its distinction from a locality, from a class structure, or from the education of its users and/or their economic condition. No matter what the motivating force, it should be encouraging to note that the number of elements that differentiate one dialect from another is small and sometimes is no more than a dozen. In contrast, the

number of identical sounds in all dialects is gratifyingly large, indicating that no matter how distinguished the dialect or the accent is the majority of word formations will rely upon already established habits of syllabification.[5] For our purposes the critical elements that differentiate one dialect or accent from another can be identified by the following terminology.

KEY SOUNDS

A critical factor in the makeup of any dialect is the way in which certain vowels, diphthongs, and consonants are pronounced. In this text, these distinctions are called *key sounds*. Here are examples:

A. Vowels. The *o* [o] in *for* [fɔr] of Standard American speech can become *fer* [fɝ] in a Midwestern dialect.[6]

B. Diphthongs. The diphthong [eɪ], as in *make* [meɪk], becomes [aɪ], as in *eye*, in Cockney, so that *make* [meɪk] is pronounced *mike* [maɪk]. Indeed, this particular substitution is used here for the simple reason that the [aɪ] for [eɪ] is one of the most prominent vocal substitutions in all the British Isles, since it is one of the marks of middle-class speech and multiple regional dialects as well and can even be heard with force as far away as Australia and New Zealand.

C. Consonants. The voiced *th* [ð] of *that* [ðæt] in Standard American speech can become *dat* [dæt] in Teutonic, Slavic, Chinese, Vietnamese, East Indian, and other dialects.

RHYTHM

The term *rhythm* is used to indicate the cadence of speech flow. However, in all but a few instances rhythm usually is indicative of a personal rather than a dialectal characteristic. For example, we speak of a person as being a fast or a slow talker or

---

[4] Jerry Blunt, *Stage Dialects* (New York: Harper & Row, 1967), p. 1.

[5] For a breakdown of this aspect of dialect study, see the Key Word Sound Drill sections of each chapter in *Stage Dialects*.

[6] The "can become" instead of "becomes" is because education, mobility, and the influence of the audible media have noticeably altered what used to be called "rural" speech, a dialect that has fewer and fewer adherents as time goes on.

of being jerky in his or her speech. The individual's temperament rather than dialectal patterns is the control factor or characteristic in such cases. In a few instances, however, rhythm or cadence is one of the characteristics of dialectal speech. American Southern is one such dialect, although how valid that distinction is today is a moot question. To grasp this last point, just recall for a moment the last few times you have heard a Southerner speak on television. In how many instances was a slow rhythm a distinct characteristic? Still, historically, the Southerner does have a reputation in this respect—one that must be taken into account in a dialectal study. In contrast, there is no question that a rapid rhythm is one of the identifiable characteristics of Jamaican speech, as you will quickly note when you listen to "Young Actress."

MELODY

The inflectional pitch pattern of a dialect gives it its melodic distinction. Again, as with rhythm, fewer rather than more dialects have notable melodic patterns. For instance, we do not think of a Dutch or an Austrian accent or an Appalachian or an English middle-class dialect as being particularly noteworthy of inflectional patterns. Some dialects, however, do feature a distinctly melodic speech and are the richer because of it, a fact made clear by the rapidity with which examples come to mind: Chicano, Welsh, Swedish, Jewish, East Indian, to name but a few.

WORD ORDER

Word order is an easily distinguishable dialectal element. However, it applies more to accents than to dialects. Mostly it is indicative of the way in which a non-English speaker has learned the new language. If, for instance, a person has acquired the new speech as a result of formal training, then certainly a part of the learning process must of necessity have involved a study of sentence structure: the relation of subject to predicate to object or the proper placement of antecedents, and so on. If the individual is a competent student and diligent in preparation, then confusing shifts in word order will not mark the person's speech. In this respect, note the command of English evidenced by many of the European political leaders when they appear on any one of our many television interview shows.

On the other hand—and this is of importance to the dialectician because it can be such a distinguishing characteristic—if the person is self-taught or is compelled to learn English from the irregular opportunities of daily living, then the person's speech most likely will feature a misarrangement of the usual word order, sometimes to the temporary loss of intelligibility. Where a teacher of grammar would react with despair in such a situation, however, the dialectician notes with pleasure the effects of such disarray and also notes, as you yourself will hereafter, how in some instances a thought is expressed with more distinction or greater depth because of that very disorder. In this respect the Greek, Yugoslavic, and one of the East Indian titles will attract your attention.

Symbols

To clarify comments about the material seen in the text and heard on the tapes, some symbols of my own, in addition to the markings of the International Phonetic Alphabet, will be used. These markings will appear in many of the transcripts immediately above the syllable, word, or phrase involved. For this purpose, adequate space has been provided between each of the lines in all the transcripts.

For the vowel, diphthong, and consonant substitutions or alterations, the regular phonetic symbols, as already demonstrated, will be used. However, where rhythm is a factor in a dialect, the rate of delivery is so immediately apparent that no marking is really needed, and none will be made. Melodic patterns are a different matter. The inflectional pattern of a single word or of two words can be quite distinctive. Noteworthy in this respect is the variation of pitch, crossing nationwide dialectal boundaries, which is heard when an English person adds two words at the end of a sentence that turn it into a question rather than a statement—a question whose purpose is almost always to include the other person or persons in what would otherwise be an individual comment. For example, "That lad wants taking down a peg or two—doesn't he?" a speaker will say, or, "Ah, the Queen was that beautiful when she came out—wasn't she?"

Then there is the lilt of Welsh speech, denoting as it does a lingering mysticism of hills and hollows and still keeping its distinctive melody in terminal words and phrases. A similar pattern is head, interestingly enough, in East Indian speech. Rather than attempt to make a mark that follows exactly the rise and fall of a pitch pattern, the single wavy line, ‿⌒∿, will be used to denote the presence of a melodic element.

ADDITIONAL SIGNS

Underlined blank spaces, parentheses, brackets, and dots also will be used to clarify parts of the transcripts.

Blank Spaces. In some instances, especially in those tapes that were recorded as much as 15 or 20 years ago, certain words or phrases remain unidentifiable no matter how many times the tape is rerun. To indicate such cases, a space is underlined and left blank in the transcript. If the listener proves more competent than the author, the lost word or phrase can be written in.

Parentheses. Parentheses are used in all the transcripts to indicate the questions and interjections of the author or the interviewer, thus distinguishing this person's words from those of the donor. These questions and comments spoken by the interviewer also appear in italics to clearly separate them from the donor's speech.

Brackets. When a question or a comment has been made by the author but for some reason—mostly that of time—has been cut from the tape, in order to let the listener-reader know what it was that motivated the donor's reply, the question or comment, unheard, has been placed in brackets.

Dots. Three dots (. . .) indicate deletions and/or breaks in continuity.

Authentic Primary Source Material

As a resource book, which offers authentic primary source material for all the dialects and accents covered, *More Stage Dialects* draws on a library of recordings accumulated at various times and in many places. All donor voices, being native, are truly representative of their regions or class. As authentic as each is, it still must be understood that there is no such thing as full uniformity among all speakers of any one dialect or accent. Variations of Cockney, for example, can be found not only between those areas north and those areas south of the Thames, but sometimes between one block of streets adjacent to another block as well. Still, it is quite proper to choose one or more individuals and designate them as authentic representatives of a particular dialect, which has been done throughout this book. Where possible—time and space permitting—more than one voice is presented in the same dialect. Some will be stronger than others, some will be more consistent, and others will be less so. Where possible, contrasts are offered. In the East Indian section, for example, an educated Hindu speaks English with the proficiency of one who has used the language from childhood on; following this are the groping phrases of an earnest student who wants so much to be able to speak the language of the land where she now lives. Both have excellent dialects, and each can serve a need.

Spontaneous Speech

To guarantee an authenticity on which the student can rely, nearly all of the donor voices were taped on location in the process of spontaneous speech, either as conversation or, as in some cases, where the subject was given to voluble utterance, in a descriptive or narrative form. In every case, the purpose was to achieve a free and unstudied delivery, the surest way to get an exact reproduction of the subject's manner of speech.

In payment for that authenticity, the student must expect to put up with the blemishes that infect any spontaneous utterance: pauses, breaks in continuity, confusion of ideas, inconclusive thoughts, and always the broken rhythm caused by the endless interjections of the ubiquitous "Ah," to say nothing of the interpolated "you know's" that presently plague English speech around the world. Fortunately, it is the distinctiveness of the sounds uttered, not the distractions, which is the target of our attention.

Additionally, if a dialect must be taped where it is found and as it is found and if, as of that moment, permission has been granted, *then the recorder and the listener must both of necessity accommodate themselves to the intrusion of unwanted background sounds,* for example, the noise of passing cars, the rattle of dishes in a hotel or a cabin kitchen, the hum of an airconditioner, or the blur of background conversation. For these and many other intrusions, there is no help if the integrity of the material is to be maintained.

Monitoring

Due to the variances of conditions when the recordings were made, volume monitoring is often necessary as vocal strength varies from speaker to speaker.

Subject Matter

Obviously, the primary purpose in the gathering of material for a resource book is to obtain matter relevant to the subject rather than to select material that will attract attention because of its entertainment value. However, it is only human to be pleased with a flow of talk that escapes being dull. More than this, if the subject matter itself is genuinely interesting, it might even be accounted a welcome bonus to the study. In my own case, even though my ear was intently engaged in performing its usual biopsy on the dialect or the accent being recorded, I found some of the material not only interesting but informative and fascinating as well (see "Constable and Bellringer"). This is to say nothing at all of the attractiveness of the personalities involved.

Prepared Transcripts

Not everything on the tapes that accompany this book is in the form of spontaneous speech. In six instances in the pages ahead, the material you will hear was read, not spoken. In every case, however, native voices did the reading.[7]

[7] It should be noted that reading is a constrained form of expression wherein the reader's own vocabulary, sentence structure, and rhythmic and melodic patterns of speech are supplanted by those of the author. However, in each of the cases presented, the distinctive sounds of the dialect are there in abundance.

1. A scene from Sheridan's *The Rivals* is offered in a North Country dialect. In this case, there is no harm. Quite the contrary is true, since the dialogue comes as freely as if it were heard in a scene onstage delivered by a fine native actor, as indeed it is.
2. The boys in the fourth form of a New Zealand school read from a fishery pamphlet. Considering our own national reputation for deficiency in all kinds of reading, let alone reading aloud and at sight, it becomes a pleasure to listen to the easy flow of these young lads in truly characteristic New Zealand speech.
3. The American-Jewish telephone conversation was taken from a previously prepared assignment.
4. An Austrian voice reads "The Red Auto" because that section of the taping session, in the kitchen of a hotel in the Alberg, was the only one not drowned out by the clatter of dishes and the calling of orders.
5. There are two short recitations, one from "Romeo and Juliet" and the other from the old poem, "Dock an' Dorris."
6. Two voices from New Mexico sound better reading "Farm Talk" than they did when they said the same thing in their own words.

Save for the above, all other taped material is in the form of free (as free as the sight of a microphone permits) and spontaneous speech.

Expedients

To achieve the spontaneity required, several expedients were necessary. The first was to tape conversations where and as chance offered—on the street, in a hotel lobby, by the side of a road—hoping for the clarity, strength, and consistency desired. If that meant leaning far out of a second-story window of an old inn, mike in hand, to record a conversation ("The Tile Man") with a worker on the roof, to coax a Missouri farmer in the middle of his cornfield to stop work long enough to tell a story ("The Tornado"), or to entice a busy Hong Kong tailor ("Salesman") to brag about his business, then that is what was done.

However, conversations between strangers, especially when one of them is holding a microphone, are not always easily begun. Accordingly, leading questions that elicited exact replies and generally dealt with the subject's locality—a useful way to obtain an exact fix on the donor's geographical location, birth, or occupation—were employed. Instances of these leading questions will be noted in the tapes that follow.

It is not always easy, once started, to keep the flow of conversation between strangers going. To this end, many short interjections ("I see," "Oh, yes," and even the lowly "Uh-huh") were used as prods to encourage and sustain a dialogue.

Names

Names are not attached to the donor voices that are heard on the tapes. There is a very simple reason for this. Embarrassed by and apologetic for their lack of proficiency in the English language, their feelings made more acute by the sight of a microphone attached to a machine that will make permanent their shortcomings, many of the donors could hardly be persuaded to talk at all. In view of the strength of their feelings, sometimes it was difficult to explain that it was their very lack of proficiency that made their speech attractive and usable. In many cases, *cooperation could only be obtained by the promise that the voice would not be identified by name.* Hence, the policy used throughout this book is one of nonidentification.

Opinions

As is so commonly and frequently stated in the media, the opinions expressed by the voices you will hear, as they speak of their experiences and beliefs, are wholly their own and do not necessarily reflect the thoughts and beliefs of those of us who produced the text and tapes of *More Stage Dialects.* Our interest centers wholly on those formal sounds that denote a specific dialect or an accent, such as might be used in the creation of a role in a play or a film. Actually, in some instances, the speaker would deliberately stop short of expressing a personal opinion on a particular subject. This was especially true for some of the Eastern Europeans when the talk involved matters of a political or an economic nature. For the most part,

however, the expression of opinions flowed freely enough; in some cases it was difficult to staunch the flow, which, of course, was all to the good as long as the distinctive sounds of the dialect were pouring forth.

Titles

It might seem presumptuous to give a title to each of the items in this source book, especially when many of them are fairly short in length. However, lest any be lost or buried in the large number of separate items offered, some clear and ready means of classification are necessary to give identity to each of the scripts. A letter or a numeral might be used, but neither would give any hint of the subject matter; a title does, hence it is used.

Length

Naturally, the time span of each separate title in the sections that follow varies as the chances and the hazards of contacting and taping the raw material differed from subject to subject. In some instances only a sentence or two could be recorded, as was the case of the Scottish woman, which was taped in a *Separate Tables* kind of English hotel, who remembered only a couple of her childhood expressions. In other cases only a few short bits of dialogue could be extracted from a longer flow, either for reasons of clarity or because the speaker's words were muted by background sounds.

Fortunately, however, there were more than enough instances in which the donor could be heard at length. Indeed, one of the most difficult tasks has been the job of editing and paring down the transcripts from a plethora of informative and interesting material to fit the limited amount of space that time on the tapes allowed.

Although it is possible to detect practically all the key sounds of a dialect within the structure of five or six sentences or, at most, a paragraph, this span alone is not sufficient for a full grasp of the subject. More than just the key sounds, as heard in word formations, is necessary to give body to a dialect. As stated earlier, rhythm (tempo of word flow) and melody (pitch inflection) are integral parts of everyone's speech and as such must be reckoned as essential characteristics of a dialect.

Consequently, each title is offered in a time

span of minutes rather than seconds to allow a fuller display of all the elements that the dialectician must deal with. There is a bonus in continuity. There can be instruction from your own memory bank when it holds a goodly quantity of stored sounds, all of which fit into the composite that makes up a dialect. Remembered phrases can and will return at odd moments much as a snatch of song does. Psychologically each return has the possibility, as happens in infancy when the child learns from what is heard, of helping articulators achieve new positions and perform difficult movements, for example, the half *b*/half *v* of Spanish, or the guttural *r* of Danish.

To obtain the benefits that added length allows, it is recommended that the student listen to each tape in its entirety as a first step in studying a new dialect. Then the student should repeat the action more than once if it is possible.[8] After an impression is implanted by the flow of the new speech, the student should turn his or her attention to the analysis of the separate dialectal units. Later, in the working sections of the book, short introductory remarks as to the clues contained in each transcript will be made, followed by examples in the text itself of what to look for in that particular dialect. However, these are only illustrations. *It is the student's responsibility to examine the text phrase by phrase and word by word and, if necessary, to mark each dialectal element so that in repeated readings not a single one will be missed.* Once the transcript has been analyzed and the individual items noted, marked, and practiced, the student's attention should be turned again to the continuity of the whole. By thus using the length of the piece to advantage, the student has the possibility of developing his or her skill as a conversationalist in the new dialect rather than becoming a mere repeater of learned patterns delivered by rote.

A Multiple-Purpose Tool

A dialect is a prime source of information for anyone engaged in the creative work of the theatre. Already apparent is the fact that it can locate a

[8] The repetition will be especially helpful in cases where the speaker, in confusion, cannot find or does not know the words with which to express himself or herself, thus producing sound rather than sense. "Polish Family" and "Nervous Actor" are good examples. Both, however, have many good key sounds to their credit.

subject not only as to national origin but to region as well. It can also disclose class status or reveal an educational background.

Further, it can and does attract attention. Seldom does it fail to get an interested and favorable response. It can add distinction to old sayings; its very presence seems to assure authenticity, whether that authenticity is there or not. It can be of some help to even the poorest story; its use in a good one is always a positive addition. Long ago humorists discovered its value and have larded their offerings with it ever since. We would be downgrading the perceptiveness and talent of our acting forebearers if we did not give them credit for using dialects long before their lines were ever chiseled in stone or written on paper. Playwrights were no less acute. Aristophanes cries for dialects; Pantalone speaks in the patois of a Venetian; Shakespeare uses dialects in play after play.

More than all this, a dialect can say much about the personality of the speaker, whether the speaker is a natural person or a character in a play. The trained ear of the dialectician, sharpened by the demand for acute perception even as it does its biopsy on the dialectal elements, can check the suggestions that are literally spilled out for his or her use in character creation. There is no better place to begin this aspect of the work than in the tapes ahead, loaded as they are, foot by foot, with all manner of clues.

There is also the element of tempo, which can be as indicative of a personal idiosyncrasy as of a regional characteristic. Is it fast, slow, or medium; is it regular or uneven; does it denote urgency or complacency, control or uncertainty? Does it have strength, the element that reveals the overall muscle tone of the speaker and the speaker's state of health? Is the tone weak, medium, or strong? Does it seek to impress the auditor or is it fearful of its own effect? Is the tonal quality pleasing or not; does a guttural quality indicate a physical condition that has been shaped by an unhealthy environment? Is there a nasal whine that tells of a disturbed relationship between husband and wife or parent and child? What does the overuse of a rich, full tone say about the speaker's ego? Does the very averageness of the total tone say something in itself?

In any case, not only does a noticeable dialect or accent attract the ear of a listener, but it informs it as well.

A Personal Book

In many ways *More Stage Dialects* is a personal book. Considering the nature of the activity itself, which always requires individual contact often made intimate by questions that encourage personal revelations, the book could hardly be otherwise. Although the actual procedure of soliciting a taped conversation sometimes brought uncomfortable or even hostile responses, such unpleasant reactions were well balanced by the large number of experiences of exactly the reverse nature. More often than not there was much pleasure involved; on many occasions a taping session led to a congenial meeting after, which could be, and often was, followed by letters and sometimes visits.

Certainly, one of the most agreeable rewards of gathering dialects is the number of friendships, some now life-long, that have resulted. As a consequence, my wife and I often feel welcome in many places around the world. In reverse, we continue to have the pleasure of hosting friends from here and abroad in our own home. A deep and abiding kinship exists with our Danish friends whether we are at our cabin by their lodge in British Columbia or they are visiting us in Los Angeles. We enjoy the recipes my wife obtained through an exchange with a chef in a Spanish kitchen. We remember with keen enjoyment not only the distinctive speech but the attractive personality of the country squire in England who at 80 still rode to hounds in his native Bucks and who hosted us with such snug comfort in a home that was young in the days of Queen Elizabeth I. It was no bad exchange either in the mountains of Yugoslavia to lose a trophy fish in order to gain a couple of good accents (not used here) instead. With anticipation we think of sitting again in the bell tower of the old church in Lavenham, England, when our constable friend helps ring the chimes for Evensong. It is a recurring pleasure to visualize having breakfast in Athens with our Greek actor friend, sitting on the roof of our little hotel in the Plaka at the foot of the Acropolis with the Erechtheum in full view, listening as he quotes appropriate lines from ancient writers in his distinctive accent.

Truly the search for and the collecting and study of dialects is an interesting and rewarding experience in itself, and that is only the bonus attached to the practice and use of dialects in the creative work of the theatre.

The Phonetic Alphabet [1]

The Sounds of the Symbols of the Phonetic Alphabet

The phonetic alphabet and the additional symbols are recorded on tape so that you may associate the symbol with the sound. To emphasize the sound being enunciated, the stress in the pronounced word is in some instances altered from the normal.

[1] It is suggested that a reference be made to the introductory remarks at the beginning of Chapter II, "The Phonetic Alphabet," in *Stage Dialects*. The material there will serve to complement the information of this section.

VOWELS

Symbol	Key Word	Phonetic Representation
[i]	eat, believe, agree	[it bə'liv ə'gri]
[ɪ]	it, think, complicity	[ɪt θɪŋk kəm'plɪsətɪ]
[e]	ate, chaotic, hurricane	[et ke'ɑtɪk 'hɝɪkən]
[ɛ]	ebb, bet, tent	[ɛb bɛt tɛnt]
[æ]	at, bat, habitat	[æt bæt 'hæbətæt]
[a]	car (Brooklynese), ask, dance	[ka ask dans]
[ɑ]	on, father, schwa	[ɑn 'fɑðɚ ʃwɑ]
[ɒ]	watch, wander, Gotham	[wɒtʃ 'wɒndɚ 'gɒθəm]
[ɔ]	ought, gnawed, Shaw	[ɔt nɔd ʃɔ]
[o]	oboe, shrove, poncho	['obo ʃrov 'pɑntʃo]
[ʊ]	umlaut, put, took	['ʊmlaut pʊt tʊk]
[u]	pool, true	[pul tɪu]
[ʌ] accented	up, above, Dutch	[ʌp ə'bʌv dʌtʃ]
[ə] unaccented the schwa vowel	*a*bove, genesis, dat*a*	[ə'bʌv dʒɛnəsɪs detə]
[ɝ] accented syllable, *r* sounded	further, bird	[fɝðɚ bɝd]

9

Symbol	Key Word	Phonetic Representation
continued		
[ɜ] accented, syllable, *r* not sounded	further, bird	[ˈfɜðə bɜt]
[ɚ] unaccented syllable, *r* sounded	further, mother	[ˈfɜðɚ ˈmʌðɚ]

DIPHTHONGS

Symbol	Key Word	Phonetic Representation
[ɪə]	beer, here, steer (Southern)	[bɪə hɪə stɪə]
[ɛə]	there, head, west (Southern)	[ðɛə hɛəd wɛəst]
[eɪ]	eight, great, weigh	[eɪt greɪt weɪ]
[aɪ]	aisle, time, cry	[aɪl taɪm kraɪ]
[aʊ]	ouch, how, allow	[aʊtʃ haʊ əˈlaʊ]
[ɔɪ]	oil, choice, employ	[ɔɪl tʃɔɪs ɪmˈplɔɪ]
[oʊ]	oat, toad, throw	[oʊt toʊd θroʊ]
[ju]	union, you, review	[ˈjunjən ju rɪˈvju]

CONSONANTS

Note that audibility is supplied to the voiceless consonants by the accompanying vowel.

Symbol	Key Word	Phonetic Representation
[p]	peep	[pip]
[b]	bob	[bɑb]
[t]	tat	[tæt]
[d]	dad	[dæd]
[k]	kick	[kɪk]
[g]	gag	[gæg]
[m]	mam	[mæm]
[n]	Nan	[næn]
[ŋ]	singing	[ˈsɪŋɪŋ]
[f]	fife	[faɪf]
[v]	vivid	[ˈvɪvɪd]
[s]	seal	[sil]
[z]	zeal	[zil]
[θ]	think	[θɪŋk]
[ð]	the, that	[ðə ðæt]
[ʃ]	sheep	[ʃip]
[ʒ]	vision	[ˈvɪʒən]
[h]	hot	[hɑt]
[r]	rear	[rɪr]
[l]	lily	[ˈlɪlɪ]
[hw]	what	[hwɑt]
[w]	watt	[wɑt]
[j]	yet	[jɛt]
[tʃ]	church	[tʃɜtʃ]
[dʒ]	judge	[dʒʌdʒ]

ADDITIONAL SYMBOLS

1. ['] A single mark indicates an accented syllable, as when *basin* becomes *ba'sin* in the Greek transcript, or *products, pro'ducts* in the Czech.
2. [:] Two dots indicate a prolonged vowel, as in an Irish *know* [no:] or a Scotch *bush* [by:ʃ]
3. [ɔ:] As heard in *ought, all, law, awful.*
4. [ʔ] The glottal stop which changes *battle* ['bætl] to [bæʔl] and *get you* to [gɛʔjə].
5. [ɛʳ] Replaces *er* [ɝ], so that *bird* [bɝd] becomes [bɛʳd] and *first* [fɝst] becomes [fɛʳst].
6. [y] Illustrated by the words *bush* [by:ʃ] and *school* [sky:l].
7. [x] As in *ach* [x], or *loch* [lɔx].
8. [ç] As in *ri-k-t* [rɪçt], or *bri-k-t* [brɪçt].
9. [β] As in *envious* [ɛnβiəs], and *vestal* ['βɛstl].
10. [/] The slash indicates a dropped sound, as when *running* becomes *runnin∅*, and *hello*, ̸h 'ello.
11. The [r] variables.²

[r] normal, as in *Missouri* or *Somerset*
[ṙ] hard, as in *Missouri* or *Somerset*
[**r**] dropped, as in *are* or *observe*
[rʳ] trilled, with *front* or *rear* of tongue
[r-l] sounded as [l], as in *from, round-and-round,* or *Moon River*
[l-r] [l] sounded as [r], as in *Los Angeles*
[lr] The two consonants, neither fully formed, are uttered in combination: *well, all, silk*

12. [〜] The wavy line indicates a variation of pitch as heard in *"isn't it?" "shouldn't they?"* and *"from me you'll hear it."*
13. [ȟ] An *h* with a check above indicates a heavily aspirated sound, as in *who,* and *Khartoum,* or *heard.*

Placement

In order not to break into the balance and the continuity of the various vocal sections of this book, the Phonetic Alphabet in Sound, with its Additional Symbols, is placed at the end of all the resource materials. In the cassettes it is placed on Side B of the second reel, and follows the last African Title #4, "Civil Engineer."

---

² Each of these variables is treated, not only in *Stage Dialects,* but in each of the sections of this book where the matter is pertinent.

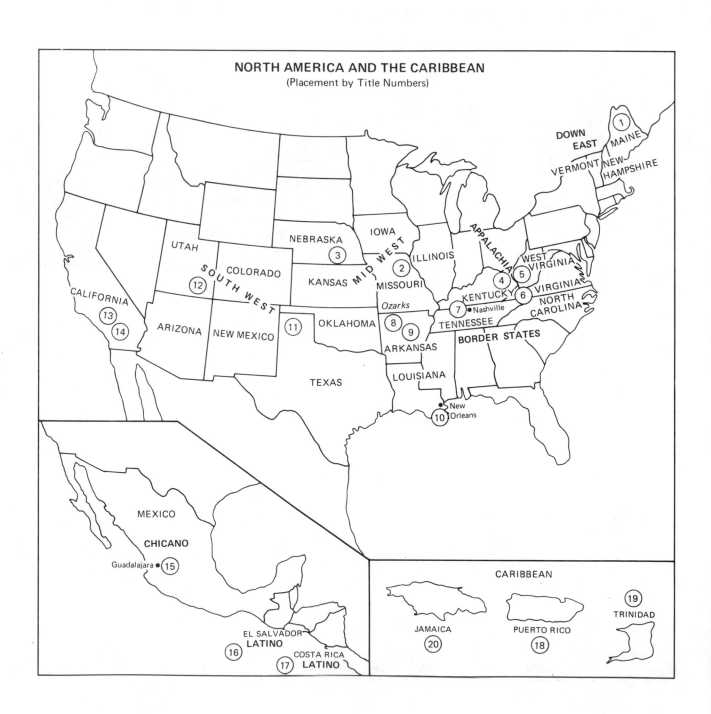

NORTH AMERICA AND THE CARIBBEAN
(Placement by Title Numbers)

North America and the Caribbean

Down East, Midwest, Border States,
Cajun, Southwest, Jewish, Chicano,
Latino, Puerto Rico, Trinidad,
Jamaica

Within the boundaries of the continental United States and the Caribbean Basin there are three major dialectal groups: Standard American speech, the ethnic accent, and the regional dialect.

Standard American Speech

The first dialectal group, Standard American, is the speech defined in our dictionaries. It is the one that is increasingly spoken throughout the country. Its creditable and prideful use by the actor is the concern of the various voice production classes in our many theatre arts departments; hence, it is not offered for study here. It is ethnic and regional speech that commands our attention in this book.

Standard American speech is of use to us in this book mainly because it is the reference source from which the other two dialectal forms derive. Unlike them, it is identified with neither a specific region nor a recognizable ethnic group. In addition, it is clearly a form of speech noticeably different from its parent speech, the spoken English of the British Isles, from which it has long been separated in time and space. In broad but simple terms, it is the dialect (any cohesive body of speech being a dialect of one sort or another) that has been created in this country by the educational process, by the steadily increasing influence of the media, and by the mobility of the citizenry. It is spoken in all parts of this country, even though it can be heard only rarely in certain isolated regions and among certain closely knit ethnic groups.

Although some in the theatre may think of Standard American speech as the poor relation of Standard English speech and, in the hope of elevating it, try to improve it by affecting an imitation of its overseas parent, it is the belief here that Standard American speech is a very good speech indeed and is capable of meeting, in degrees from adequate to brilliant, our communicative needs, among which the demands of the theatre are not least.

Representing the standard or norm, Standard American speech does not have the distinctiveness that the extensions or extremes of regional or ethnic speech possess. This fact, however, does it no harm because its effectiveness is not limited in either utilitarian or aesthetic expression; it can guarantee full force for the blunt statement just as well as it can weave a web of subtlety around a devious thought. Furthermore, it will bear the burden of beauty that any poet, from Shakespeare to Frost, can impose upon it. Certainly, it will reward the skillful user as much as any speech can.

The Ethnic Accent

The second dialectal group is composed of and is formed by the speech of those persons whose parent language was not English and whose pronunciations, language structure, vocabulary, and inflectional patterns reveal a first language of foreign origin. This form of speech is denoted here as an accent, the strength or weakness of which is determined by the degree of influence of the original oral language. A strong accent, if it is clearly understood (and legitimate to a role), is generally preferred by actors and audiences alike.

Because of the heterogeneity of our population, it is to be expected that as many different accents can be heard here as abroad and with as much, often more, strength and distinctiveness.[1] The catalogue of such accents is long and global in scope, including all of Western and Eastern

[1] See Chapter 6, Western Europe.

Europe, Africa, the Middle East, and Asia as well. So numerous is the mix, that it became a matter of minor importance as to whether one or another of these accents would be placed in this section or be placed in the section that discusses its native region. An arbitrary decision, determined in part by the timing requirements of the tapes, was made that places the Swedish, Slavic, and Chinese accents, for example, in the non-American sections and the Jewish, Chicano (Spanish), and Cajun in this section. Obviously, there was no distinction made in the taping itself, since each source was gratefully recorded whether it was found here or abroad.

The Regional Dialect

The third dialectal grouping, the regional dialect, is found throughout this country and is richly endowed with usable dramatic qualities. As the map on page 12 indicates, it is spread from north to south and coast to coast. Further, each separate dialect is noticeably different and distinctively attractive, offering playwright and player alike a rich body of material to use in the creative process. Unfortunately, it is a fragile source.

Even though in some areas regional dialects seem sturdy and resolute, their integrity is being endangered by the mobility that, year after year, allows alien workers, retirees, and tourists alike to spread into all parts of the country. At the same time, on a daily basis, the influence of education and the media acts to erode the distinctiveness of these regional dialects. For some of us who believe that a restricted uniformity of pronunciation and idiom will be harmful to the interpretive process, the loss of a Yankee, a Midwestern, or a Border-state dialect will be serious indeed. To the end that they and other dialects and accents will not be allowed to disappear, this resource book makes its contribution.

CANADA

Standard Canadian speech is almost identical to Standard American speech. The difference,

mainly, is in the use of two diphthongs: [eɪ] and [ɛʊ]. The Canadian [eɪ] replaces the American [aɪ] and is heard in such words as *right*, *like*, *might*, and *night*, and the Canadian [ɛʊ] is substituted for the American [aʊ] and can be heard in *out*, *about*, *house*, *south*, and so on. In addition, *been* [bɪn] or [bɛn] *might* be pronounced [bin] in Canada, just as *either* ['iðɚ] and *neither* ['niðɚ] possibly can be sounded as ['aɪðɚ] and ['naɪðɚ]. So also, *again* [ə'gɛn] *might* be [ə'gen].

Aside from these noticeable differences, since the similarity of the vast majority of pronunciations and inflections in the speech of the two countries is so marked, it is not necessary to allot time on tape for a separate Canadian chapter in itself. This is not to say that the whole range of Canadian speech is not as rich and as varied in foreign accents (French Canadian and all the other European, Western, Eastern, and Asiatic as well) and regional dialects (Standard English, Cockney, Scottish, Irish, etc.) as is our own. Indeed, several of the dialects and accents offered in this book were taped north of the border, the fidelity of the material being as certain there as here.

DOWN EAST

Maine, New Hampshire, Vermont

It is appropriate to begin the United States section of *More Stage Dialects* with a representation of the Down East speech of Maine, New Hampshire, and Vermont, not only for geographical reasons (located as the area is in the extreme northeastern section of the Atlantic seaboard) but also because it is one of the oldest and probably the hardiest of all our country's dialects. The distinctiveness of this speech will be apparent in the very first sentences heard on the tape, made so by (1) a delivery that exhibits a character all its own, unlike any other in our country and (2) a series of key sounds that also are unlike most of those heard elsewhere throughout this country.

Cultural continuity and climate are the two principal conditioners in the Down East dialect's formation. Its long history is one of slow adapta-

tion of the original speech brought into the area by the first English settlers, which was altered only little by the intrusion of Irish and Italian settlers to the south in Massachusetts and not at all by the presence of the French in the north beyond the Height of Land in northern Maine. Climate and location determined the principal occupations of the area—forestry, agriculture, and fishing—none of which required a large quantity of verbal communication for successful practice.

Consequently, Down East or Yankee speech, both dialect and delivery, is sparse, even to the extent that it allows a fact to speak for itself with little verbal adornment, and it is deliberate and slow. It is also purposeful, a kind of speech that lends itself to laconic sayings and that has established a reputation through the years for embodying rustic wisdom. Several popular plays, written in the last century, did much to sponsor this last characteristic. They were plays that featured a rustic hero (Ezekial Homespun, Solomon Swap, and Asa Trenchard) whose native acumen always allowed him to get the better of any city slicker. Always in control, such a character can be imagined as speaking between tight jaws and thin lips, indicating frugality in the expenditure of both energy and words.

More than most other dialects, the pace and tone of a Down East accent is expressive of attitudes. This will be heard in our script in the inflected endings of several phrases and sentences and should be considered as much a characteristic of the dialect as of an individual trait.

Here are the principal key sounds of the dialect:

1. As usual, the phoneme [r] is made prominent, first by being unsounded [ɾ], as in the words *first*, *letter*, and *Bar Harbor*, and then by being made somewhat harder than usual, as in *interesting* and *warrant*. Further, a terminal [r] can be added, although it is not so featured in this script, in the recognizable way that makes *idear* out of *idea* or *Ader* out of *Ada*.

2. The *g* of *ing* can be dropped, [g̶], an action that does not occur as often as it well might in this title, which would change *responding*, *receiving*, and *living* to *respondin'*, *receivin'*, and *livin'*.

3. One of the most distinctive and usable key sounds in Yankee speech is the often used [ɪə] ending, heard here in any number of words: *here*, *other*, *remember*, *player*, *series*, and so forth.

4. Equally distinctive is the long [u:], as heard in *you, through,* and *use*.

5. A broad [ɑ], heard in *half* and *can't*, is used with a vigor seldom matched anywhere else in the United States.

6. Certain colloquial words, not heard in this script, are distinctive and can be used to advantage: *ayeah* for *yes; wunt* [wʌnt] for *want* or *won't;* and the rural *fer* for *for, git* for *get, wuz* for *was,* and so forth.

Title #1: The donor in the following selection, a native of Maine's easternmost county, provides us with a distinctive and very usable dialect. In pronunciation and delivery, it is neither too rustic nor too stock.

Town Meeting

. . . Responding to your various letters, ah, as I wrote to you about a month ago, upon receiving your first letter, I had given it some thought when the entire Atlantic Ocean kinda swept through my living room. . . . So finally I hope that I can, ah, get some things down here that you might be able to use. If you can't, don't worry about it. In any event I will, I will run on to some extent on the first side here, and you can select what you can use, and what you can't use, you can make Christmas ornaments of, or something.

I was born in the town of Cherryfield which, ah, ironically is the blueberry capital of the world, or so we bill ourselves. Now Cherryfield is not too far from Bar Harbor, ah, it's about halfway between Elsworth, about half way between Elsworth and Machias. Now Machias is interesting, or has an interesting history, because it was in Machias that the first naval battle of the American Revolution was, was fought. Ah, now whether that little bit of history will orient you or not, I don't know. But if it doesn't, it won't hurt anything.

[The subject matter changes.] You know, town meetings are kind of interesting things. This past town meeting, for example, I remember a little bit of an altercation that occurred between Gordon Tibetts, who was in the audience, ah, and who was perusing his Town Warrant when all of a sudden he came upon, ah, a bit of information that somewhat upset him. It seems, well anyway, Gordon got up in the meeting and said, "Mr. Moderator," he was addressing Fred Nealand who was usually the moderator of the town meeting, he said, "Fred, Fred, says here in the Town Warrant that, ah—we'll call her Mary Jones for anonymity's sake—it cost the town, I think it was $250 for Mary Jones to have her illegitimate baby. Now, is that right, Mr. Moderator?"

And Fred perused his town report a minute, he said, "Yes, yes, I guess you're right, Gordon, I think it did, yeah." "Well," Gordon said, "now if you'll turn to page 46, it says here that, ah, the town of Cherryfield was paid $275 by the father of that child in repayment." And Fred looked through his Town Warrant on that particular page and said, "Yeah, yeah, I, I guess you're right, Gordon." "Well," Gordon said, "you know, Fred, I'll tell you something. It looks to me as if the town made a profit of $25 on that deal." Gordon [Fred] said, "Yeah, yeah, I guess you could say that." "Well," Gordon said, "you know, Fred, before I sit down, I've got a suggestion. Don't you think it might profit the town to breed her again?"

MIDWEST

The American Midwest, where some of the best speech in the country is spoken, is also the heartland of one of our most distinctive and pervasive dialects, that is, as much as it can be pervasive in the face of the growing uniformity of standardized speech that has spread and is spreading throughout the whole country. Indeed, the clinging on of the old dialect and the insurgence of the new provide contrasts that can be heard side by side, or syllable by syllable, in the same broad area whenever parents and children or the old and the young talk together, which proves that education and the media today are more powerful factors in the formation of vocal patterns than is the influence of home or parent.

What was once a widespread and relatively uniform manner of speech is now a decreasing phenomenon, which is all the more reason for preserving it. For there is no mistaking this fact: Midwestern speech, embracing the Ohio, Mississippi, and Missouri river basins, embodied a vocal language that in vocabulary and utterance was a mirror of the lives and occupations of its users. In farm and town, in kitchen, country store, and rural classroom, the speech was as plain as the clothes the people wore and as utilitarian as their tools.

It was, of course, a mixture of the syllabic formations spoken by the pioneers who poured into the area throughout the eighteenth and nineteenth centuries. In some cases, where the influx into a particular area was homogeneous, as was that of the Scandinavians into the North Central states, the dialect took on a character all its own. In the main, however, a common vocabulary and pronunciation pervaded the whole area. It was a rural, practical, nonspeculative speech, sometimes sounding as flat to the ear as the surrounding land appeared to the eye, and in the beginning it was uneducated, all of which gave it its distinctive character. That it should be preserved as an artifact of national importance goes without saying.

Most dialects or accents have a certain number of detectable key sounds that are used consistently in the speech of that region. Midwestern speech, however, in contrast to American Southern, for example, does not have a proscribed set of vowels or consonants that appear with regularity in given circumstances; the dialect is more flexible than that, but it does have several other elements that define its character.

One of these characteristics is a colloquialism of pronunciation that is applied to certain short, common words. Here is a partial list in which the colloquial word is linked to its standard mate: *git—get; fer—for; wuz—was; ever—every; jist—just* or *dist—just, dis—just; cuz—cause; becuz—*

because; cain't—can't; ain't—aren't; hisself—himself; hit—it; chimley (chimbley)—chimney; thang—thing; thank—think; effin—if, and many more.[2]

Another characteristic is the addition of a vowel *a*, sounded as [ə], to the front of the present participle while the final consonant *g* is dropped: thus, *running* becomes *a-runnin'* and *laughing* becomes *a-laughin'*. Further, there is a tendency to lengthen vowels, not consistently but often enough to be detectable, as will be heard in the words *east, field,* and *round*. Certainly, no other key sound is more characteristic of Midwestern speech than the muscular tightness that can be heard in its hard *r* [ř]; if you pronounce *bear* as *bar*, you would hear what I mean. In addition, verb tenses are often made notable by their misuse.

[2] In the last several decades these colloquialisms as they were pronounced in the past have been less and less in evidence throughout the area. Yet, no farther back than the 1930s, 1940s, and into the 1950s it was to be expected that in a beginning voice classes in theatre departments, even as far off as California, there would be a couple or even half a dozen students who would still use these colloquialisms.

Title #2, Missouri: The following conversation was taped on a summer's day while we were standing between the rows of a Missouri cornfield. A slight breeze registers on the microphone from time to time.

The Tornado

VERBS⟶

. . . I seen one, one in daylight. It never done any—well it done some damage, but it didn't kill anybody or—(*What, what did it look like?*) Oh, just, just a cloud with a big funnel hanging down out of it. (*In other words, just looked like the pictures you see, huh?*) Yea, uh-huh. Ah, this one in particular come about three o'clock in the afternoon, and it come out of the southwest and it hit a barn, tore this barn up, and then turned and went east, well, about a mile, it stopped, just stood still down there over a field, and that tail just go round and round and whipped back just like a, a whip sometimes—(a cat's tail)—and just hanging down there—(*I thought they always had to keep moving.*) No, this 'un stopped, and just stood

there. The cloud, excepting that tail in the bottom of it, the cloud just set up there

in the air and that tail hung down and it was just switching back and forth, I guess

it was making up its mind which way it wanted to go, and finally it took off east and

went across the river, there was a place over there had a row of big pine trees, oh,

must have been as long as from here to the highway, great big pine trees, and it

took right up the side, up the south side of them trees, and it looked like it just took

a chain saw and just cut ever limb off over to the body of the tree, where it just

went straight up. It just took ever limb, twig, everything off them trees. It just

sheered 'er down just as slick as a rib. (*And left, but left the trunk?*) Left the trunk,

the trees standing there and the limbs on the other side. . . . And that woman had

about one hundred and fifty laying hens, and them chickens running round down

there next day, not a feather in 'em. It pulled ever feather out of them chickens,

they're just as bare as a spanked baby.

Title #3: In the next selection an enthusiastic fisherman talks about one of
his best fishing holes. Note the continual use of the vowel [ɪ] (it) in the
first two sentences in *against* and *can* and its elongation in *big* and *fishes*.
The *r* is hard [ř], but some of the other sounds are quite soft, even
melodious.

Nebraska Fisherman

. . . Throw that old plastic worm up against it, though, and see if we can't catch

us another one of those big fish. I know we can. Doggone, I wish every bass

fisherman would have, have an opportunity to get into something like that. I know a

lot of 'em, a lot of you have possibly done even better than that, but, ah, well then

they are in there that size to catch, and when they're biting that hard, you're not

going to have any, any trouble catching a few of 'em.

And seems like the better places there are to, ah, ah, fish in these areas, the

more brush there is. And this is the meanest bass, the hardest fighting,

large-mouth bass I have ever fished for. I'm not just saying that, now doggone,

you ask someone else who's been down there, and they'll tell you that they'll, that

they will literally jerk the rod out of your hand when they hit a plastic worm.

THE BORDER STATES

Appalachia (Kentucky, West Virginia, Virginia), Tennessee, Ozark-Arkansas

The term Border States was created originally in the mid-1800s as a political description of those areas that lay between the solid North and the equally solid South, each of the states containing at times an indeterminable mixture of the attitudes and practices of the neighbor that lay on one side or the other. In the sense that these areas still are open to influences that press upon them from both the North (or Midwest) and the South, the designation is as aptly usable by us as a dialectal term today as it was earlier as a political and economic one. The regional pronunciations of both the Midwest and the South vigorously meet and mix in a Border-state speech, which is as distinctive and attractive as any other in our country.

In some instances, of course, the influence of one neighbor or the other predominates, as Title #7, "Country Music," and Title #8, "The Woodworker," demonstrate. In others, there will be an almost equal mix.

As might be expected, the phoneme *r* figures prominently in Border-state speech, either by its use or disuse. Where the Midwestern influence prevails, it is sounded vigorously [ř]; on the other hand, it can be softened or dropped, as it is in a Southern dialect. Many instances of both will be heard in the following tapes. In addition, in a fairly unusual circumstance, the hard *r* [ř] of the Midwest can be heard directly next to a typically

Southern syllabic sound, for example, when the diphthong [ɔw] comes before [ř] in the word *north* [nɔwřθ] (Title #9, Arkansas, "Travel Information").

Other typical Midwestern or Northern key sounds will be heard in the pronunciation of such words as *wuz, fer, git,* and so on, as well as a mix of verb tenses and antecedent nouns and pronouns. On the other hand, the Southern influence will be heard shortly when [ɪ], as in *it,* is substituted for [ɛ], as in *eh,* in such words as *ten* [tɪn], *then* [ðɪn], *cents* [sɪnts], and so on. It also will be heard when those Southern diphthongs [aɪ], [ɛɪ], or [æɪ] and [æɔ], [æə], [ɔw], or [uə] produce their lengthening and sometimes softening effect, as in *right, take, ask, go, down, all, book, egg,* and so forth.

Of unusual interest is the duplication heard in multiple instances of the typically Cockney and English middle-class diphthong [aɪ]. One of the most used of all syllables in English regional speech, the [aɪ] is heard in equal abundance in Border-state pronunciations. That the latter is a direct descendant of the former is most unlikely and hardly acceptable, even as an interesting speculation; certainly such a theory is not advanced here. Still, in the colonization of our continent, there was a notable influx of British settlers into what is now Appalachia, Kentucky, and Tennessee, and it is a fact that some of the sayings and songs of the mountain people as late as the 1910s and 1920s were closer to the speech of, say, Elizabethan times than any other speech then practiced in the English-speaking world. Isolated then, as the people still are in part today, and free from the pressure of other pronunciations, the speech could have retained old sounds down through the years. (It is at least an interesting speculation when we think today how easily a transplanted Cockney would recognize some of the sounds of Border-state speech, especially when he or she hears the repeated use of *thang* for *thing* and *thank* for *think*.)

Finally, in the case where the Southern influence prevails, a Border-state speech should not neglect the ever-present expressions of "No, sir," "Yes, sir," and "Y'all come back," which lend an unmistakably polite feeling to any ordinary conversation.

Appalachia

The three titles in the Appalachia series progress geographically from north to south, following the narrow, twisting, and often rutted roads (coal trucks) down through the "hollers" from Kentucky and West Virginia into northwestern Virginia itself. One of the donor voices was born and raised very close to the little town that is quite appropriately called Appalachia.

Title #4, Kentucky: The first short transcript features a hard *r* [ř] and the common mispronunciations and mixed grammar that so marked the speech of the early settlers as they moved westward down along the Ohio River—sounds that still are heard in strength, as this first donor demonstrates. In one instance, the donor almost uses the old-time colloquial pronunciation that makes *best here* sound like *best cheer*. A Southern influence, less pronounced, still can be heard in the diphthongs [eɪ] in *maple* and [æɪ] in *pine* and *mine;* also heard is the [ɪ] that replaces [ɛ] in Tennessee [tɪnə'siː]. The furniture-maker talks of the woods he uses and the customers he services. The sibilant *s* is an individual characteristic.

Furniture-Maker

(*What woods do you use?*) . . . You got your cedar and maple, pine, oak, most of—most of mine now comes out of Tennessee, of course the wood comes [from] all over the country, out of this country, out of Tennessee. (*What makes up the best, do you think?*) Cedar is what I sell the best here. I sell oak and maple, the three top sellers here. And then black pine is still a good seller, comes along with it.

(*You service this whole area then around through here?*) As much of it as I can get the business out of. (*What all do you serve? Doesn't look like there are any houses around here.*) Ah, there's plenty of people. There's thirty some families lives in that holler over here. About a hundred in this holler right down here half a mile going left hand. All these hollers is full of people. Plenty of people around here.

(*What do they do back in the hollers?*) Ah, they just mostly live back there. They come out and work different places, travel, some of them travel as high as fifty mile to work, as far as fifty. (*What kind of work do they do? Is it coal?*) Anything and everything, coalmine, bookkeep, you got ever—all kind of people here, does all kinds of work.

Title #5, West Virginia: The donor in the following selection lived in a "holler" in the hills at a point about half way, north to south, through the often mine-scarred Appalachian Mountains. His speech reflects his geographical position. The sounds of work in a coal mine office are heard in the background. He begins with a bald statement of fact.

Coal Country

. . . This is coal country, c-o-a-l, coal mining is our chief industry in this area. It's, ah, bituminous coal, a soft coal a, most of it is metallurgical coal—(*What do you mean?*)—used for making steel.

The coal lays like a, a river bed, or what it's just like a ocean. It just lays flat, thirty inches thick or six inches thick, through, through the mountain. It could be ten-twenty miles wide, and all the way through the mountain, it could be one hundred miles through the mountain, wherever it outcrops or surfaces on the other side of the mountain . . .

I was born right here in an old log house, and the log house still stands at this time, people are living in it right today. [Your father?] He was a coal miner. Chiefly that's what most everbody does. Eventually all industry or everything livelihood depends on coal mining in this country.

Title #6, Virginia: The donor in the following selection is truly on the southern side of the Appalachian Mountains, as the presence and strength of the typical Southern diphthongs so indicate, as does also the substitution of [ɪ] for [ɛ]. Colloquialisms such as the dropped *g* of *ing* and the substitution of *d* for *j* in *just* are quite apparent. It is to be noted that although the *r* is not slurred or dropped in Southern style, neither is it given the hard pronunciation that is so characteristic of much Midwestern speech.

A college student, this donor protested that this recording was undoing much of the work of her speech instructor. The taping was done in the Green Room of the theatre building where, incidentally, the drama students were presenting *Separate Tables* and doing an outstanding job of overlaying their Appalachian dialects with the required Standard English speech of the play.

Social Worker

I'm from Big Stone Gap. I go to school at Clinch Valley College where I'm a senior and I'll graduate in May, and I will begin work at Heritage Hall Nursing Home in Big Stone Gap, where I'll be working with elderly patients.

Ah, it'll be—I'll be called the Director of Recreation, but there'll be a lot of social work involved in it, ah, basically occupying the time of the patients to, you know, taking them to town on shopping trips, ah, providing arts and crafts for them, ah, taking them on outings, like going fishing and ah, ah, you know, just anything that interests them that we can, you know, work into the schedule that, you know, ah, it's not dangerous, you know, like we wanted to take them hunting one time, and they wouldn't let us do that because it's too dangerous, but they, you know, we can take them fishing and things like that, on hikes. (*Old people on hikes?*) Yes, short hikes. . .

Title #7, Tennessee: In Nashville, Tennessee, no conversational subject could be more topical than country music. In addition to the key sounds previously discussed, note the presence and the strength of the [aɪ] and [ɛɪ] diphthongs. The hum of an air conditioner, unwanted but unavoidable, is heard in the background.

Country Music

(*Why do you like country music?*) Well, it comes from the heart, it really does. I think a lot of people that sing country really, you know, they, they really get into their music. I think, ah, just they're not just singing a song, they're expressing their feelings. A lot of people write on their, on their really, their, their lives, like Dolly Parton, for instance. She wrote "The Coat of Many Colors," and she was a poor girl from, ah, around Tennessee, yes, and she was real poor and she wrote about a coat of many colors that her mother made for her. And her mother sewed, ah, patches together, you know, to make her coat, and she was really, you know, happy about it. And now that she's a big success, she wants people to, to understand how a poor country girl lives.

[She had just listened to a playback of our conversation.] OK, well, like the sound of my voice comes, well, they come from the heart, but when you hear it from a tape recorder, ah, it comes back and you're saying, well, is this really me, is this the way I express my, my feelings toward, you know, to other people, by my talking? You can express your feelings from your, your smile, from your face, but when you talk it, I think that, ah, well, really, it comes from, comes from your heart, and people listen, you know, to your voice, and you're saying, well, ah, is this really me, talking like this? And when it comes back to you, you're saying, well, my gracious, is this really me, you know?

Ozark-Arkansas

The comments previously made about the dialects of the other Border States are equally pertinent here.

Title #8, Ozark: The donor of the following transcript, born and raised in the Ozark Mountains, was taped in his shop, talking as he worked with draw-knife and plane to shape the parts of the chair ("cheer") he was making. While there is a Border-state mix in his key sounds, obviously the Midwest influence predominates.

The Woodworker

. . . this is hickory, (uh-huh) it's hard to work. Now the chairs and stools that I make, I use hand tools all the way through. Naturally I want a wood that will work good. Another thing, if you—when hickory dries out, you don't make anything with it with hand tools. As far as making chairs is concerned, when I get the bark offen this, this is pure-de waste. Of course now they'll take it up here and use it [to] barbecue meat with. (*Oh, sure.*) If I was at home, I'd made firewood out of it. But, you know, I'm just thinking as far as making chairs is concerned.

. . . Yes, mam. Now, you see when I get this bark dressed down like I want it, it's soft and pliable. You can weave it in the chair seat that day. Now this will start to peeling in the spring of the year when buds begin to swell and show color, a good average in this year in this area is around the 15th of April. Now it will peel like this up until about the 1st of July. Now, what happens then, the reason it quits peeling, this layer of inner bark on the timber, not only hickory but all of it, this and the tree itself start growing together, and between that time and the following spring, this layer of bark, like I'm apeeling off now, will actually become this year's growth of wood. And while that's taking place, between this outside bark and this layer, there's a new layer [of] bark agrowing. Now when spring comes that process is all completed. The tree has another growth ring on it, and I have a new layer of bark to start with.

Title #9, Arkansas: **The willing and helpful donor in the next transcript, stationed at the information desk of one of the state's well-appointed Travel Bureaus, offers a dialect that is almost classic in its strength and** consistency. To indicate its fullness, phonetic notations are given for the first two sentences.

Travel Information

aɪ   √ aɪ   √ æɘʊ ɖ   æɘʊ ɔw æɘʊ ɪ   √ æɪ ɘ   √
OK, you're right here now, and if you go on down ten more miles from here at

æɪ   ɖ ɪ   ɔw aɪ aɪ ɪ   ɔw√   √ aɪ æɘ   ɪɘ
Alma and get off on Highway Seventy-One North. We're right at the foothill of the

√ æɘʊ   ɪ   ɔw√   aɪ ɘ aɪ
Ozark Mountains, and this Seventy-One North will take you right through the

√ →
Ozarks. You stay right on Seventy-One up to Rogers and get off on Highway

Sixty-Two, and then you start out on Sixty-Two and it takes you all around this

Beaver Lake area—they have all kinds of resorts, you know, camping, whatever.

And then it runs you right into Eureka Springs.

Eureka Springs is known as the Little Switzerland of America, and it's a real

interesting little town. It's built in this mountain where the streets never do cross

each other, they just keep on winding around and round. And in the summer time

they have the Passion Play there, it's an outdoor theatre type of play.

And then stay on Sixty-Two and it will run you into Sixty-Five. And in Harrison

you can come down Highway Seven, and Highway Seven is rated by the Triple A

as one of the top ten scenic drives in the United States, a beautiful drive. And we

have at Jasper a diamond cave that can be toured. And above Jasper we have

Dogpatch—now it's not open right now, but that's where they have like Little Abner

and Daisy Mae.

And you might want to come on over at Harrison on Sixty-Five and then come

down Sixty-Five and take Highway Sixty-Six off of it, and it will take you over to

Mountain View. Now that's where they're having a folk festival right now, this

weekend. And they make all kinds of arts and crafts up there and have like country

music. And right by that we have our Blanchard Springs Caverns which is one of the largest living caves in North America, and they can be toured also. And then

you can come on down Sixty-Five and it will run you back into the Interstate Forty,

if you was going out toward Memphis.

CAJUN

Of all the dialects or accents spoken in the United States, the Cajun patois is the most individual, as well as the most distinctive, because it stands more nearly as a language within itself than does any other. Its origins are known: When the English forcibly deported the French inhabitants of Arcadia (Nova Scotia) in 1755, one group made its way to Bayou Teche beside the Mississippi River in what is now the state of Louisiana. There they and their descendants remained. In the years since, the orig-inal French language was subject to a unique series of influences, namely from the English, Spanish, Indian, and African populations that sur-rounded and pressed in upon the area. The result is the Cajun dialect, a speech barely understand-able to outsiders when it is spoken in full strength. As with all languages, however, modifications have been made to accommodate communication with the present English-speaking people of the area. These are the modifications that you will hear on the accompanying tape.

Title #10: Some of the key sounds of the accent to listen for are:

1. *d* for the voiced *th* [ð], for example, *dis* for *this* or *dey* for *they*
2. *t* for the voiceless *th* [θ], for example, *tousand* for *thousand*
3. the dropped *g* of *ing*
4. a *d* for *t*, for example, *liddle* for *little*
5. the omission of many consonants and the partial formation of others
6. the rural pronunciation of *git, fer, 'cuz, hep (help),* and so on
7. as heard in the stories, grammatical alterations turned into colloquialisms
8. the traditional French substitution of [i], as in *eat*, for [ɪ], as in *it*, for example, *ees* for *is* and *leesten* for *listen*
9. an *s* substituted for *z*, for example, [wɑs] instead of [wɑz]

The donor in the following selection, highly educated, returns to the speech of her youth in two stages. The first is with medium strength as she describes the life of her native town. The second, the Cajun story, is in full strength—pronunciations, colloquialisms, and all. The phonetic notation is given in the story.

Cajun Tales

. . . I'm from Donaldsonville, Louisiana. It's a little town on the Mississippi River,

about seven thousand people. (*And you grew up there?*) Yes, I moved there when

I was five years old, and lived there until I was about seventeen. (*What was life like in that particular area?*) It was easy, it was a good life. It was a small town, it was friendly. The food was good, the living was easy. (*You had many friends there, grew up with them?*) Oh, yes. They still my friends. I go back and I see them every year, and they don't change. Other people change, but people from Donaldsonville, Louisiana, they don't change.

(*Now what was that story you were telling me?*) Oh, the story of Little Hood Riding Red. One day, ah, Little Hood Riding Red's mama call her and she say, "Little Hood Riding Red, your mama across the swamp is sick to bed. You brung her some crawfish bisque." So Little Hood Riding Red now she put on her cape, she get in her pirogue, she paddle, paddle, paddle down the ba'you.

Pretty soon from behind a tree come this big old wolf. He say, "Hey, child, now where you going?" She say, "Oh, Mr. Wolf, I going across the swamp to see my mama who's sick to bed. I going to brung her some crawfish bisque." And that wolf said, "Man, I love that crawfish bisque." She said, "I got to be going, Mr. Wolf." So she get back in her pirogue, she paddle, paddle, paddle down the bayou.

Pretty soon she come to her mama's house. [Knock] "Who there?" "Mama, it's Little Hood Riding Red. I come brung you some crawfish bisque." "I love that crawfish bisque. Come in, child." So Little Hood Riding Red, now she walked in, she see her mama lying in bed, and she said, "Oh, Mama, now what big eyes you got." And her mama said, "All the better to see you with, child." She said, "But, Mama, now what big ears you got." Her mama say, "All the better to hear you with, child." And then she [said], "But, Mama, now what big teeth you got." Her mama said, "Oh, you like that? $5.98, Sears Roebuck!"

SOUTHWEST

This region, as large in area as the Midwest and as much of an approximation as the latter, spreads from parts of Arkansas and Oklahoma through the Texas Panhandle and across New Mexico and into Arizona. The dialect has many elements—key sounds, colloquial expressions, and verb problems—in common with Midwestern speech, the influence of Southern pronunciations causing one of the main differences. There is no trace of influence by the Chicano accent, which is prevalent (and has been since the earliest times) throughout most of the area. The phonetic transcription is in the second script.

Title #11, the Panhandle: There are two donors in the following selection, both of whom read from a script. Although the free flow of dialogue is lacking, the key sounds of the dialect are there. The second voice takes up where the first leaves off. The area is northern New Mexico, which is close to the Texas Panhandle.

Farm Talk

[This here is] an example of how a person would talk if he come from somewhere in that big stretch of farming country that goes from Texas up through Oklahoma to the wheat states like Kansas and Nebraska and as far north as Montana. I don't mean to say that everybody you come across in them places is going to sound like this here, but you sure will come across a lot of them that will.

Maybe it's farm talk, I don't know, because this way of speaking sure does follow the big prairie grass country that stretches from north to south on the west side of the Mississippi. There is just hundreds of miles of it, and it produces some of the best steers and some of the best grain, and some of the finest folks in this here country. My paw and mama come from there, of course they ain't—of course they ain't there now, because they got caught up in that dust bowl to-do back in the '30s. You've heard about that, I'm pretty sure.

[Second voice with more Southern influence in the speech,] That was when the sun got hot and there wasn't any rain for months on end and the winds come up and blowed all the dust away. Folks lost everything they had, a whole lifetime of

hard work, of sweating and praying that just blowed off down the road. Course

things is better now since that time twenty and more year ago. The farmers learned

how to plant and to plow so as to cut down on erosion, and right now that whole

section is producing so much wheat and other stuff that it has got to be stored

away as surplus. Times sure do change, don't they? Anyhow, I'm right glad that

things is better than they used to be. I guess a lot of folks are.

Title #12, Southwest: The donor's speech in the following selection is an
excellent example of the dialect of the area; although it is not extreme, it
still is strong and consistent. Mixed with the hard [ř] is the softness of
Southern sounds. One of the distinctive things to note is the tendency to
flatten some of the front vowels, not to the extent that a full substitution
is made but to the extent that it still affects a subtle alteration, as heard in
the words *ten, twelve,* and *now.* Also, there is an elongation of other
vowels, as in *know, made,* and *time.* The pronunciation of *just* together
with the hard [ř] makes a strong connection with the Midwestern dialect.

This transcript was taped in the Four Corners area of the Southwest.
The steady hum in the background comes from an air conditioner.

Sand Paintings

[Before the speaker spoke about sand paintings, he repeated a little story told

some years before when I was in the area.] Well, this was back a few years ago.

This sounds like a Texas story, but it was in the newspaper and it is true. They had

a picture of it. But ever morning this little girl would go out on the porch with a

glass of milk and a spoon, and her mother had no idea of what it was for until one

morning she went out and seen her and fainted herself, because the little girl was

feeding a rattlesnake the milk through a spoon, and they did get a picture of it and

they did have it in the papers, so evidently it is true.

(*Would you tell me about the sand paintings?*) Well, the sand paintings were

originally, as you know, a tradition. They weren't on the market up until about ten

years ago, approximately twelve now, I guess. . . . They'll never complete a sand painting. As far as you and I—(*not even the ones we buy here?*) True. We don't

know what's left out and we don't know why that it's not completed other than it's

against their religion.

(*Now who is it that makes the sand paintings?*) Well, now it's the—we have

quite a few making sand paintings where before they was put on the market, it was

only made by medicine men, which it was made, ah, for instance, once a year we

have a nine-day ceremonial here. The first day they start the sand painting. Each

day they add to it. At the end of the ninth day, before the sun goes down, when

they complete the sand painting, then the patient, the patient is standing right

beside when the medicine man will take a portion, a very small portion of each

color sand, put it in a little pouch, and then the patient is required to set down in

the sand painting, which destroys the whole thing, because it is made with loose

sand—and then, of course, that has to [be done] become before the sun goes

down.

JEWISH

It would be quite proper to list many Jewish accents under a European heading, as Austrian, German, Polish, or Russian. It would also be correct, in those instances in which the Yiddish language itself is the main influence upon spoken English, to leave off the modifier and just say a Jewish dialect or a Jewish accent. Both of these conditions are included here; further, both are listed, not as American regional dialects, which they are not, even though they are surrounded by those dialects in this book, but as accents spoken in the United States and heard daily in many of our major cities. As it happens, both of the following transcripts were taped in Los Angeles, although neither accent originated there.

This is a speech rich in all the components of a good accent: key sounds, melodic inflections, and rhythmic patterns. Of key sounds, more will be heard here than in most of our transcripts, and interestingly enough, it will be found that some vowels not only substitute for others in the normal way but often replace each other, for example, an [ɛ] (*eh*) for an [æ] (*at*) in *and* [ɛnd] and then, in reverse, an [æ] for an [ɛ], as in *telling* [ˈtælɪŋg].

Other vowel substitutions to note are: [i] (*eat*) for [ɪ] (*it*), heard in *dinners*; [ɑ] (*father*) for [ʌ] (*up*), in *mother*, and in reverse, [ʌ] for [ɑ] as heard in *college*.

Consonant substitutions are numerous and active: [d] for the voiced *th* [ð], [v] for [w]; [g] added to *ing* [ɪŋg]; a back-throat roll to the [rʳ]; and a strongly aspirated [h̃], like a muscular rasp in the lower throat.

The melodic inflections and rhythmic patterns are distinctive and often are heard together in the same phrase; a wavy line ⌇ indicates the variations in pitch. Listen for "From me you'll hear it," in Title #14.

Title #13: The donor in the following selection, an expert dialectician in her own right, offers one of the few prepared transcripts in the book. The value of it is that it provides an almost complete catalogue of the key sounds involved as well as vocal suggestions of melodic inflections. In addition, it represents a Jewish accent that is directly related to the Yiddish language, unmarked by any obvious influence of European speech. As such, it stands as a model for the speech of a very large body of the Jewish population in the United States.

The foreign words used can be translated thus:

noshing—eating, snacking
yarmulkahs—skull caps
Brucheh—blessing, prayer
nu—well, so
kvetching—complaining
kvelling—feeling pride
vay iz mear—God help me
goy—a non-Jew
schlepping—working hard, especially caring
shmatas—raggedy clothes
Gay gizinterhate—go in good health

On the Phone

ɑ   v   ɪ ə   t   i
Hello, Moishe, we have a good connection here? Good. Listen, Moishe, I'm

æ ŋg   æ ə ʌ   væ   ɑd   d vʌ   d ŋg
telling you I'll never forget it. Last Wednesday my mother and father were sitting,

ŋg   æ v d   ŋg   rʳ   i
noshing matzos, gefilte fish, anyways they're talking about Friday night dinners.

ʌ   h   d   i   t rʳ
You know, how important and beautiful it is to start the Sabbath right. Just at

d æ   d   d   d   d ɛ   d
sundown, the men put on their *yarmulkahs*, the mother lights the candles, says the

æ ŋg d   d   ɛ d   d ɛ li   də ɛ
blessing, father says the *Brucheh,* and then all the family is together, and eating,

ə   →
and it's lovely.

Every Friday night, as we were growing up, we always observed the Sabbath.

But now that my brother, you know, Sol, is away at college, well, we really miss

him! And that is what Mamma and Poppa were saying. That for almost a whole

year Sol has not been home, even for Friday night dinners.

And then, out of the blue, in the middle of all their *kvetching,* the phone rings, and who should be on the other end—it's Sol! "Hello! He's coming home for the weekend. He'll be home in time for Friday dinner and, it shouldn't be a total loss, he'd like to bring a young lady to meet the family."

Well, when they finally hung up the phone, my parents were beaming. *Kvelling?* They were so filled with love and pride, *oy,* their buttons were popping off their shirts. Their own *mensch!* Their big man!

And then Mamma stops suddenly and she says, "*Vay iz mear,* I didn't even ask if this lady is Jewish!" Poppa says, "What are you talking? Would Sol bring home a *goy?*" Mamma says, "Who knows, in these modern days."

And for a moment they were stumped. All the *schlepping* they had done to raise Sol—all those *shmatas* Mamma had worn in order to save money for the children, they should grow to be well and go to college. Then they stopped again and each caught a glimmer in the other's eyes, and Mamma says it out loud, "*Gay gizinterhate,* our Sol, our beautiful, intelligent son, will bring home some kind of human being—no matter what kind. Who are we to judge? This will be a human being because that's our Sol. He wants us to meet a person, and that's good enough for me."

And hearing all this, Moishe, I am so happy at their understanding that I hug them and I kiss them, and get this, Moishe, I even cry a little bit—me!

Title #14: The donor of the following selection, in the United States since 1914, still shows the influence of another language on her Jewish accent. For all the strength of her speech, there are remarkably few key sounds in proportion to the number of words spoken. However, sooner or later, most of the key sounds do appear. More obvious are the melodic patterns evidenced throughout the transcript, some showing considerable variety, others being sustained on a nearly constant level, both of which are indicative of a major characteristic. The rapid tempo and the rush of phrases are individual traits; for the actor such rapidity requires a good deal of caution.

The Star of David

. . . My family lived, I show you some pictures—they, they live in Moscow. We have a family plot in Moscow in the cemetery and, on one side is the Jewish, and one, the non-Jewish. And on the Jewish side you see they had the Menorahs, they had the praying hand, you know, they, they—the candelabras, or they have a Star of David.

You see, a Star of David is not religion, it's not a cross, you know—with the Star of David is—is when the King David went to battle, and the six-pointed star was on the shield, on the battle shield. And what is that we, we worship so much King David, because he went on battles and never shed a bit of blood to us, no bloodshed—thou shalt not kill—because he had the Round Table discussion, King David did that. They call him the blue-eyed and pink cheek. He settled the battles around the Round Table, the boundaries without shedding blood. And that why we, we—we think of him with awe, what a king he was. And that why we have the Star of David—six-pointed star. Now you get the story. You didn't know the real story? From me you'll hear it. . .

[The subject was prayers in school during her childhood in Russia.] Well, I would make feel like two cents. You see, in Russia the boys sat in one classroom and the girls in the other. Ah, in the morning the teacher said, those that don't believe in Christ shouldn't go on their knees to pray and cross themselves, but they should stand up. So it was myself and my girl friend and three other little girls. We stood up. But we knew what we'll get when we get out by recess. They circled—the children circled around us like a pack of wolves, and everybody spit in our faces, and my, my little dress, and the other kids', were wet with spit, and I went through hell all the years with the prayer in school.

SPANISH IN AMERICA

Chicano, Latino

The meeting and mix of Spanish and English in America seems to have a dynamic all its own. When an interplay takes place between the two, a vigorous, exciting, and attractive accent results, as the next several transcripts demonstrate.

There are millions of Chicanos and Latinos (Americans of Spanish descent) in our Pacific Southwest. A very large number of them—professors, doctors, lawyers, actors, and so forth—speak an English that is indistinguishable from the best speech in the area. On the other hand, many speak no English at all. In between is a large body of persons whose conversational range varies from a verbal flow that reveals just a hint of an accent to one that shows a struggle with both vocabulary and pronunciation.

The donors of the following transcripts all live in the United States and represent both Mexico (Chicano) and Central America (Latino). They belong to a middle group who in word choice, word order, and pronunciation function quite well between the two extremes mentioned.

In a Chicano or a Latino accent, the first element to be noted is the presence of the key sounds of the Romance languages (Spanish, French, and Italian): the [i], as in *eat*, for the [ɪ], as in *it*; the trilled [rʳ]; the [d] for the voiced *th* [ð]; an [s] instead of a [z], which changes [wɑz] into [wɑs]; an occasional dropped [ɦ]; the substitution of [ʒ], as in *vision* ['vɪʒən], for the [dʒ], as in George [dʒɔrdʒ], making [ʒɔrʒ].

Distinctive of the Spanish accent itself are these other key sounds: an occasional reverse of the Romance language substitution of [i] (*eat*) for [ɪ] (*it*), for example, *each* changed to *itch* or *piece* to *pis*; the addition of the vowel [ɛ] (*eh*) to the beginning of a word that starts with *s*, for example, *starts* changed to *estarts*, *speak* to *espeak*, or *Spain* to *Espain*; a *d* placed before some words that begin with *y*, notably *yes* changed to *dyes* [djɛs] or *you* to *dyou* [dju]; the voiced *th* [ð] substituted for *d*, so that *San Salvador* becomes *San Salvathor*; a broad *a* [ɑ] replacing other vowels, as heard in the words *mother*, *one*, and *parents*; another vowel, the [ɔ], as in *ought*, which does the same thing and is heard in the words *others*, *under*, and *work*. Quite distinctive also is the alteration of the consonant *v*, changing it to a half *v*/half *b*, designated by the phonetic symbol [β]. It is formed, not by placing the lower lip against the upper teeth, as in making a normal *v*, but by almost touching the upper lip with the lower, as for *b*. Listen for this key sound in "Guillermo Temblece."

Title #15, Chicano: The donor of the following transcript represents a good cross section of the Chicano accent, which is easily understood and yet is unmistakably Chicano. The key sounds to listen for are those just mentioned. One element that is not demonstrated in this transcript is the melodic inflection that sometimes comes at the end of a sentence and is best illustrated by the somewhat stock expression, "I think." Although it is often overdone, the inflection is a legitimate device to use in the Chicano accent.

The Mechanic

Well, I was, I was born in Juaroz, woll, nearby, about twenty miles from there—

lived there for most of my life, but then I went to Texas, El Paso, and lived there for

a few years, just across the border anyway. And I then came to, to Los Angeles with my family. (*How long have you been here in Los Angeles?*) Well, I was here

really two different times. Once I was here for about two years. Ah, this time I have

been here for about three and a half years.

(*What do you plan to do here in Los Angeles?*) Well, I was—I was thinking to try

to get, to get a good job and I have to learn a trade, and my brother is a mechanic

and he told me that I could, you know, work with him to learn something about how

to, you know, to work with these cars that I fool around with, but I don't know

enough to, you know, to make this my living. (*Do you like being with cars?*) Oh,

yeah, I like to, I like to, you know, get a car, you know, buy an old car and I get to

fix it up, sometimes I can make a couple of hundred dollars, you know, after I fix it

up. But I got two cars now that I don't want to give 'em up or nothing, they're so

cool, you know, because, eh, I, you know, the way that we fix these cars—. . . .

(*Have you thought of going on to school?*) Well, that's what I was planning to

do, you know, they got a good trade school here, and I was planning to go to

school in El Paso, you know, and eh, ah, I don't know, I have to work and it was

really too hard. But then I had to stop, eh, in the, the last job and I had to quit that

job. I came here and now I plan to go to the L.A. Trade Tech, you know. Is a, is a

good school, and they teach you to work on cars, and get experience from—you

learn how to do it by actually doing it, and I think that's the best way.

Title #16, Latino **(Costa Rica):** The accent of the donor in the following
transcript shows in typical style how a new speech develops when it is
acquired informally in a learn-as-you-go process, which comes from a
need to communicate at work, in a store, or on the street. The result is a
kind of undisciplined accent that sometimes emphasizes a key sound and
sometimes does not. Such a haphazard process is one of the distinctive
qualities of the speech.

There is a further interesting dichotomy in this donor's delivery: a
flexibility of enunciation results in some very clear syllabic formations
that are matched shortly after with such a slurring that two words rapidly
become one. This element, together with a fascinating word order
arrangement, makes for a most enjoyable and usable transcript.

My Good Name

. . . but I born in Costa Rica—I come from Costa Rica. (*How long have you been here in Los Angeles?*) Oh, I been here by six years, yeah, about that. (*Is your family in Costa Rica?*) Yeah. (*How many people in your family?*) Oh—in all the family? (*Yes*) I cannot tell you. (*Father, mother?*) Oh, you say in the more near? The near is about seven. (*Seven—father, mother, brothers, sisters?*) Yeah, my father, my mother, ah, my two sisters, ah, one baby, ah, that's all in my—(*Where do they live in Costa Rica?*) No, no, this—my parents, they move to El Salvador. (*To where?*) El Salvador. The others, they live in Costa Rica—my aunts, uncles—. . .

I student. I come into Los Angeles City College to try to get a career, to diploma, because I has working here in United States in many different, ah, in many different kind a—(*work?*) the work, the labor. And a, this is better to with a career, with a diploma is better, you know because is—I was working the postal, ah, is hard and low wage, because the more you do, more they want, and they pay piece work, and it's terrible, you know. I was working construction, is same. (*Working what?*) Construction work, (*Ah, yes*) I was working the joiner in the tower, the shipyard in San Pedro. They pay good, but I feel—I don't feel good. It's a continually same daily. I prefer to get a career and come back to these places. I left my good name and come back to positions, any position there, maybe in the office—account, or general business.

(*And what are you studying now?*) Eh, by the moment I am, eh, I try to get the more English what I can. I have a—develop communication—communications, Speech 40, and another class, only in relative with English. But maybe in the next semester, semester—maybe in the next semester I start to get, ah, Business 1, or Accounting 3 to start to get something in the career—. . .

[I asked him to repeat some of the sounds.] Yeah, I say "d'you," I don't say "you." We say "d'yesterday." "D'you"—yeah, we because, ah, we the way we read is the way we pronounce, and is hard to start, to start to put attention in this word—to talk too botter, I put emphasis in—in put attention in what I talk to. But when I need to talk too fast, that is the same way of old time. (*You—you go back to the old habit.*) Yeah.

Title #17, Latino (***El Salvador***): The donor of the following selection, as did the previous one, follows the pattern of key sounds mentioned at the beginning of this series and in the same irregular manner. Especially note the last sentence.

Paratrooper

Well, original I was born in Spain, and my parents went to Central America, and so I was living in San Salvador, El Salvador. (*In where?*) San Salvador, El Salvador. (*How long?*) For ten year. (*Go to school there?*) Yeah, I was going to school and I graduate, ah, from, ah, secretary, and after I went to the Air Force, and I was three year—(*You were a pilot?*) No, I was the paratrooper. (*You were a paratrooper?*) Uh-huh. (*In what country?*) El Salvador. (*You are a sky diver?*) Yeah, yes, I am.

(*Will you tell me about sky diving? Do you like it?*) Oh, I love it! (*What do you do?*) Well, there are two kind of jumps. One is, ah, we call, ah, combat, and the other is free fall. The combat, they, they use just for sight and, ah, the other one is more, how can I say—In the sky diving, when the, ah, well, ah, at the time that we have to jump, the instructor start to count and say that if we are ready, so when we say "yes," ah, he say, "OK, go out, jump!" And we go out and we count until four and, ah, and we check that the parachute has to be open and, ah, after that takes around one minute to, to hit the ground. [*How do you hit the ground?*] With the legs together, and we have to bend the body a little bit and, ah, turn, turn around so the parachute like, for example, if there is a wind, there is windy, you know, the wind cannot go inside the canopy, and could be dangerous.

THE CARIBBEAN

Puerto Rico, Trinidad, Jamaica

Title #18, ***Puerto Rico:*** The donor of the following selection, a Puerto Rican and an award winning actor, gives us a transcript that differs somewhat from the usual. The accent, however, is as true as it is attractive. The situation is a mock interview. An actor, Manual Lavor, has just come in to read for a role.

Guillermo Temblece

(*Ah, tell me, Mr. Lavor, ah, what have you prepared for us?*) Ah, well, I have something here that is by a—is a Puerto Rican playwright and he's, ah, Guillermo—*¿cómo se dice?*—in, in a English is a Guillermo Temblece. (*I beg your pardon—I don't think that's a—what country is he from?*) Oh, he's from *Inglaterra.* (*Oh, England! He's an English playwright?*) Well, yes, that's what they say, but I know he's really Puerto Rican, but they say—(*How did you find—how did you find his, his plays?*) His translations are all over the worlds! (*What is his last name?*) In Spanish, is Temblece. (*Temblece?*) Yes, you know, when you go like this, you go like that—(*You shiver?*) No-no-no-no, when you—(*Shake?*) Shake, shake, yes.

(*Manuel, are you talking about William Shakespeare?*) That's him, the same fellows. You know him, too? He's not bad, you know that? (*OK*) OK, here we go—

But soft, what light through yonder window breaks?

It is the East and Juliet is the sun.

Arise fair Sun and kill the envious Moon,

Who is already sick and pale with grief

That thou her maid art far more fair than she.

Be not her maid, since she is envious,

Her vestal livery is but sick and green,

And none but fools do wear it, cast it off

(*Juliet enters at the window.*)

It is my lady! Oh, it is my love!

Oh, that she knew she were!

She speaks, yet she says nothing. What of that?

Her eye discourses, I will answer it.

I am too bold, 'tis not to me she speaks.

Two of the fairest stars in all the heaven,

Having some business, do entreat her eyes

To twinkle in their spheres till they return . . .

Juliet, aye me!

(*Thank you very much—*) Thank you. (*It's been a pleasure—*) Lavor, Manuel

Lavor. (*Lavor*) Lavorrrrrrr.

Title #19, Trinidad: The donor of the following selection, an actor who created the lead role in an important new play, in the process of being interviewed suddenly dropped into character and continued the dialogue, accent and all, in that form. He began with a couple of snatches from an old folk song. The accent itself shows the influence of an African background on all native speech. There is, however, a limited number of key sounds to be considered: an [i] (*eat*) for [ɪ] (*it*), a [d] for the voiced *th* [ð], and, notably, a stressed [en] for the unstressed [ɪn] in the word *mountain*. A stressed final syllable that normally is unstressed is another characteristic of the accent, for example, *my'self, moun'tain, val'ley,* and *ug'ly,* as is also the limited vocabulary. The heavy, plodding tempo is a character rhythm, not an integral part of the accent.

The Charcoal Burner's Dream

Mooma, mooma,

Your son in the jail already,

Your son in the jail already,

Take a towel and bind your belly.

Mooma, mooma,

I pass by the police station,

I pass by the police station,

Take a towel and bind your belly.

I my'self was born on Sur Morne, Mt. Taque (?), which is, a, ah, you call, a
moun'tain in San Lucia up in a, you, ah, where the people come from Trinidad.
[*Trinidad?*] Well, I live on the moun'tain. I, I come down sometime, Trinidad—the
people in the val'ley, they live—they Trinidad. (*And your background?*) My
background? My—I not—I no remember my mother, no my father. My background
was the mountain, and the charcoal—

[*And your dream?*] Oh, I dream, I dream I would wake up and find me down the

mountain and across the sea. You see, a woman come from, she come in my

dream, the woman in dream tell me I was king, a lion, not what they say, ugly, like

the macaque, you know, that is monkey face, and they say I have monkey face, I

am not a monkey, this woman tell me in dream.

Before all the other people say I ugly, and they throw stones at me, and they—if

I go down, they dogs, they set them to bark at me. I never look in pool water, no

mirror because I don't want to look at what they see. Then this lady appear, when

the moon was out, and she came out of the moon and finally she was standing

right there in front of me. And she have come enough time so I no—I no have to

believe what the people say anymore, because now she tell me I no devil, but I

have now angel talking to me.

So, yes, I believe her because I feel better. (*She is an angel?*) Eh—she woman.

I never have woman before. I not have her, but she, she sleep with me—eh, she,

she angel.

Title #20, **Jamaica:** At a theatre conference, as I was standing in a hallway following a morning session, the speech of a young woman attracted my attention. I introduced myself and shortly thereafter taped the Jamaican accent of the donor.

The first characteristic of this accent is its rapid tempo, a pace that is, according to the speaker, relatively slow in comparison with that of her friends at home in Jamaica. The second characteristic is the sustained pitch level, made more noticeable by a sharp clipping of consonants. Next, there is an habitual altering of emphasis or stress, which will be heard in *Kingstown* and *Jamaica.*

The major key sound change, as the donor herself notes, is a dependence on the vowel [ɑ], as in *father.* In addition, the *g* of *ing* is dropped while an interesting insertion is made of the [æ], as in *at,* in the word *theatre.*

Young Actress

(*Would you tell me where you are from?*) Yes, I was born in Kings' town, Jamai' ca. I have been in the States for over a year now. And I am presently going to Moorpark Col' lege. And I am a Theatre Arts ma' jor, with my minor in psycholo' gy. And I am very interes' ted in working in the theatre. I have come to the conference in order to meet more people and learn more about the theatre arts.

[*Would you tell me something about your speech background in relation to that of your friends at home?*] Yes, if I was to see some of my friends in the country, they would sound more like—[here she explains her own problems]—I am working hard and slowing down my language, and theirs is much faster. Right now I am, as you can tell, that's when I am really trying to make a point, I will slow down. And that is what I am doing right now. But they don't, they just keep right on talking.

[As for her own background—] I took speech, to learn how to say the words. In our country, *a* [e] is not pronounced *a,* it is [ɑ] [as in *father*] sound. And I would have say, like—it's hardly to go back and pick it up now. I have tried to lose it for so long. Ah, but since I have been in the United States, that would be a good way to say it, ah, I have learned how to use the *a* [e] sound more, because we don't, the *a* is more of an [ɑ]. And that is what I am working on now.

I am presently in two plays. One of them is "Annie Get Your Gun," at the Conejo Players, and "The River Niger," to where I have to lose my accent altogether. And what I do is listen to people talk and watch the way their lips go. And I am able to learn it that way. I listen to a lot of tapes, and I will watch peoples' face or features and see how they move their lips. And then I will go home and I will work on it that way. Ah—(*Do you work in front of a mirror?*) Oh, yes, I have to, because that is the only way that you can see your lips move. And that is what I am trying to do, is to move my lips in the same way. I don't know how to get rid of the accent that is behind. It's been with me for so long.

THE BRITISH ISLES, AUSTRALIA, AND NEW ZEALAND
(Placement by Title Numbers)

The British Isles

England, Wales, Ireland, Scotland

The four major dialects of the British Isles, Standard English, Cockney, Irish (literary Ireland and Dublin), and Scots (literary Scotland and Edinburgh), are covered in depth in *Stage Dialects* and are not duplicated here.

To those four, this book adds some of the notable regional dialects of the British Isles. After three examples of London speech, the dialect trail leaves the capital for the north of England where the provincial tour begins. It then descends through some of the middle, eastern, and southern counties before moving into Wales. After Wales comes a dialect tour of Ireland followed by a crossing into Scotland with passage through Glasgow for the Glaswegian speech of the Scottish Lowlands. Then up into the "Hielands" and the far reaches of Wester Ross.

ENGLAND

Breaking the sequence of north to south the tapes of the English dialects offer several minutes of what *might* be called middle-class speech. Now, today in Britain stating what is and what is not middle-class speech is very much like asking a

psychologist to tell us exactly what is and what is not normal. At best it can be said that middle-class speech is an entity that has very ragged edges of definition, as English speech patterns demonstrate. Granted that social, economic, and educational barriers do exist in Britain, still the lines of distinction are very wavy indeed, with nothing like the rigidity that used to exist, say, before World War II.

For one thing, World War II did heavy injury to all facets of British life. Wartime stresses broke down all kinds of distinctions, both in the armed forces abroad and in the populace at home; the breaking might have been forced, but, in true British style, it was shared. Mobility was marked. This meant that one set of distinctive speech sounds came flat up against other ones that were just as distinctive; daily contact softened the edges. Since this first major breakdown of vocal barriers, continued mobility, plus the influence of education and the media, have further eroded distinctions.

Still, dialectal differences do exist and are heard in abundance throughout the country, each sustaining its individuality with dogged insistence. Even when changes occur in inherited speech patterns, lingering evidences of an original dialect can be heard which offer telltale evidence of who the individuals are and where they came from. It is very usual, for instance, when a distinguished scientist is being interviewed on television to hear not only the learned speech of his or her schooling (Standard English) but some of the key sounds of the scientist's original dialect as well. Unlike former times, he or she probably is not in the least disturbed by the mix.[1]

One thing must be noted about each of the voices you will hear on the tapes: all the donors are British and all are *likely* to share the following common pronunciations:

1. The broad *a* [ɑ] that produces the English *demand* [dɪmɑnd] in contrast to the American *demand* [dɪmænd] is one such, and there are nearly 200 other words that fall in this category.

2. Another typically English vowel sound is a fuller, more rounded *o* [ɔː] than is heard when Americans pronounce the *o* in *ought* [ɔt], which for them becomes [ɔːt].[2] The letters *a* and *o* are the ones that are used the most to carry this particular sound, as in *all, law, ought, awful,* and *pause.*

3. To form the English diphthong [ou], Americans must stretch it into a triphthong [ʌou], adding a barely perceptible *uh* [ʌ] first. In *Stage Dialects,* I call this the *so don't go* diphthong because those three words contain the same vowel combinations. *Over, holy, omit, told, most, moment,* and *tone* are other typical words that carry this sound.

[1] The one key sound most likely to be heard is the diphthong that changes *make* [mek] into *mike* [maɪk], *place* [ples] into *plaice* [plaɪs], or *rain* [ren] into *rine* [raɪn].
[2] Drop your jaw, place your tongue as if to say *o,* and then close your lips in a restrained circle and enlarge your upper throat as you sound the vowel.

4. Most English people soften or drop an *r* when it comes before a consonant: *short* [ʃɔːt], *word* [wɜd], and *hard* [hɑːd]. Or they drop it and replace it with *uh* [ə], thus: *year* [jɪə], *there* [ðɛə], *empire* [ˈɛmpaɪə], *your* [juə], or [jɔːə].

5. Certain words receive a pronunciation that differs from ours. Some of the principal ones are: *again* [əˈgen], *been* [bin], *either* [ˈaɪðə], *neither* [ˈnaɪðə] (none of these four are universally so pronounced), *clerk* [klɑːk], *Derby* [ˈdɑːbɪ], *figure* [ˈfɪgə], *hostile* [ˈhɔstaɪl], *issue* [ˈɪsu], *laboratory* [ləˈbɔrətrɪ], *nephew* [ˈnɛvju], *patent* [ˈpetnt], *privacy* [ˈprɪvəsɪ], *process* [ˈprosɛs], *schedule* [ˈʃɛdjul], and *virile* [ˈvɪraɪl]. In addition, most English people (and this can be heard as far away as Australia and New Zealand) elide sounds when they pronounce yearly dates, thus: *nine-teen-four-teen* (1914) becomes *nine-een-four-teen* or *eight-teen-hun-dred* (1800) becomes *eight-een-hun-dred.*

It is appropriate that the series of tapes on English dialects should begin in the city of London. The following three titles, before the regional dialect trail begins in the North, are offered as a representation, somewhere near the middle of the enormous spread of vocal patterns that can be heard daily throughout the capital. The two opposite ends of the dialectal span, Standard English and Cockney, are not covered here.[3]

Due to the variance of conditions when the recordings were made, volume monitoring is needed for certain titles in this section, for example, the volume needs to be increased for "The Rivals" and decreased for "The Pilot."

[3] See Jerry Blunt, *Stage Dialects* (New York: Harper & Row, 1967).

Title #1, Central London: The first title comes as close to being representative of a broad spectrum of middle-class speech as any in this book, and it is chosen to open the section for this reason. It is less distinctive than any of the regional dialects offered, most of which, incidentally, are also middle class in background, for example, a bookseller, a constable, a city council member, a hotel manager, and so on.

Of all the dialects offered, the one presented in "Housey-Housey" requires the least amount of change in the speech of an American actor and probably would be the most understood by an American audience. It stands nicely balanced between the extremes of Standard English and Cockney and would serve very well in a number of plays.

The donor was an official in a car transport firm. At the outset the very widely used diphthong [aɪ] is heard in the word *played* [plaɪd], giving an excellent contrast to the American pronunciation of [pleɪd]. A second key sound follows quickly: the glottal stop (not as full bodied as it obviously was in the donor's youth), which speaks of a Cockney background. Equally suggestive of a Cockney background is the pronunciation of the first word uttered, *Well,* in which the *l* is not as fully sounded as it should be. The slurred or softened *r* in *army* and *preferred* is another key sound to be noted, as is the triphthong [ʌou] in *Tombola.*

Housey-Housey

[There was a question about the game of Bingo.] Well, yes, I played it quite a lot

when I was in the army, and we—we preferred to call it "Housey-Housey," or

"Tombola," which are two other names for the game. (*What was that first one,*

"Housey-Housey?") "Housey-Housey," yes. I don't know—I don't know how it got

the name of Housey-Housey. Except, of course, that when you get a—you play, you

know, you—you get a card with fifteen figures on it in three lines of five, you see,

and you play for a line. When you—when you've won, you shout "House!" (*Ah,*

that's how—) That's probably how they got the name Housey-Housey, you know.

(*We yell "Bingo!"*) Yes, that's right. The idea is basically the same as Bingo . . .

We have a lot of expressions that go with the numbers. For instance, ah, #9 is

referred to as Doctor's Chum. Ah, this is because, ah, in jokes, in the past, ah, a

pill known as a #9 has been prescribed by doctors for such things as

constipation, and that sort of thing. Of course, thirteen is unlucky, that's

international, isn't it? (*Yes*) Ah, can I think of any more off-hand? Yes, there is one,

88. This is variously called—ah—well, the most common one I've heard is Two Fat

Wafs, you know, the Wafs—(*Yes*)—the Women's Air Force, ah, and 88, if you look

at 88, it does look like two rather round figures. (*How do the Wafs feel about*

this?) Well, I don't know. Let's see if—well, 45 is halfway, isn't it—four and five,

halfway, is halfway between 1 and 90. All the 7s are variously known as either crutches, because two 7s look like a pair of crutches or walking sticks—all the 7s,

Walking Sticks is one expression I've heard. Then there are other things. Sixty-six

is referred to as Clickety-Click. This is supposed to be derived from somebody that

tried to say 66 and had false teeth that were loose fitting.

Title #2, Central London: The donor's key sounds in this title offer another
clear and effective representation of the loose entity I have called
middle-class speech. The scene is metropolitan London and the speaker is
commenting in a public session on an economic program just published
by the government in power.

Together with the expected vocal formations is evidence of a
glottal stop, a Cockney characteristic that has leeched its way
upward—socially and economically—into other speech forms. Also to be
heard, as a Cockney influence, is the flattened sound of an elongated
vowel, for example, the [æ:] in the word *about*. This is balanced by the
exceptionally strong [ɔː], as in *boards*, of Standard English. Note the two
pronunciations of *been:* [biːn] first and then [bɪn]. This inconsistency is
quite usual throughout the country.

Parliamentary Review

. . .—being the last one to speak there's not a lot left to say, but I think the

emphasis on the word neutral was his theme throughout, and this is obviously what

he's been aiming for. The increase, ah, the subsidy of 10 million's for the rates. I

don't think this is going to make a great effect in rents, although this could be

effective right through the board.

I'd like to learn a little bit more about this land-holding charge, whether this is

going to apply to buildings that have been built for speculative gain. And being a

nondrinker, I'm not too perturbed about the spirits. But it's obvious that this

bloody-ruddy tax is not going to make any decrease there. He's still going to have

his pound of flesh out of that. Ah, the pensions—very pleased to see this, although

again rather light.

Children's shoes? Well, it just shows what campaigning can do. Ah, fortunately

he, ah, there are several areas been left to this bloody-ruddy (?) tax which will still feel the pinch, and this is probably where prices will be reflected by sharp

practices in certain sectors.

Title #3, Southwark: The next title is offered to connect a so-called middle-class speech with the untutored accents of a widely spaced body of vocal patterns that are termed, in this instance, Cockney. The dialect actually is a mix that crosses the upper and lower borders between those who have had a medium amount of education and are of average means ("Parliamentary Review") and those who are not that privileged.

On a dialect gathering mission, cruising by bus and by foot in Southward (pronounced by a quick merging of syllables as 'Sou-thark), I heard the accompanying dialogue as it was being filmed, apparently for a television commentary program, on the sidewalk beside a newly renovated housing project. A small but orderly crowd had gathered and stood silently watching. Not so quiet were the dogs. The speaker gestured to an exposed section of studding in a downstairs wall of a semidetached villa.

This donor's speech may seem strong in contrast to the previous voice, but when it is compared with that of a true Cockney, such as the lorry driver taped on the banks of the Thames and reproduced in *Stage Dialects*, it is lucid indeed.

Housing

   . . . You have these joists put in in pairs to support the walls, the party walls upstairs, and the central—the chap [who] has put the central heating in has cut a nine-inch section out of two of these to get his duct in, and of course this has weakened it to such an extent that the whole lot is just caving in into the center . . . →

There is absolutely nothing right, the way this house has been built. I've got the

same trouble upstairs with the walls. There's—there's basically, there is no support

for the walls upstairs, and at the moment a lot of people deny it, but there is

immediate danger, I think. The bedroom walls in one of my kiddie's rooms only

needs a good shove and that's down. Well, no—actually without any exaggeration,

I'm getting lumps of brick falling out . . . so I thought it naturally was made of

rubbish.

Title #4, North Country: Of all regional dialects, none is richer in full-bodied sounds than England's North Country, which undoubtedly accounts for its popularity. No only is the idiom most distinct, it is also equally attractive to the ear. Several counties or shires make up the area: Northumberland, Durham, Cumberland, Westmoreland, Yorkshire, and Lancashire. Of these, dialectically speaking, Yorkshire and Lancashire are the best known, and between them the former is more popular than the latter. Both, however, are exceedingly interesting to work with and pleasing to hear and use.

Of all the key sounds of a North-Country dialect, one stands out as the most identifyingly distinctive. It is known and immediately recognized by practically everyone in the country, and there are two words with which it is associated more than any others. To say *by gum* [ba gum] or *luv* [luv] is automatically to place yourself in one of the northern counties, most probably Yorkshire.

Distinctive also is the melodic pattern that will be noted in this transcript. It will be heard immediately in *wouldn't do it, kingdom,* and *a mind to.* The key sound of [a] in *staff* differs from the Standard English of the broad [a] in the same word [stɑf]. Also the [ɔ:], as in *all,* does not appear, nor does the much used [aɪ], as in *rine* for *rain.*

In this particular reading, it should be noted that the nasal quality used is the result of the actor's interpretation and is not to be taken as a standard dialectal characterization of the region.

The Rivals, Act IV, Scene 1

RICHARD BRINDSLEY SHERIDAN

DAVID: Ah, by gum, sir! I wouldn't do it. There's not a Sir Lucius O'Trigger in the kingdom should make me fight, when I wasn't a mind to. Oons! what will the old lady say when she hears o't!

ACRES: Oh! David, if you had heard Sir Lucius!—Odds sparks and flames! he would have rous'd your valour.

DAVID: No, no, indeed. I hates such bloodthirsty cormorants. Look'ee, Master, if you'd wanted a bout at boxing, quarter-staff, or short-staff, I should never be the man to bid you cry off: but for your curst sharps and snaps, I never knew any good to come of 'em.

ACRES: But my *honour,* David, my *honour!* I must be very careful of my honour.

DAVID: Aye, by the Mass! and I would be very careful of it; and I think in return my

honour couldn't do no less than to be very careful of me.

ACRES: Odds blades! David, no gentleman will ever risk the loss of his honour!

DAVID: I say then, it would be but civil in honour never to risk the loss of the

gentleman.—Lookee, Master, this honour seems to me to be a marvelous false

friend; aye, truly, a very courtier-like servant.—Put the case, I was a gentleman

which, thank God, no one can say of me; well—my honour makes me quarrel

with another gentleman of my acquaintance.—So—we fight. Well, that's

pleasant enough. Boh!—I kill him—Well, that's my luck. Now, I ask you, who

gets the profit of it?—Why, my honour.—But put the case that he kills me!—by

gum! I go to the worms, and my honour whips over to my enemy!

ACRES: No, David—in that case your honour follows you to the grave.

DAVID: Now, that's just the place I could make a shift to do without it.

ACRES: David, you're a coward!—It doesn't become my valour to listen to

you.—What, shall I disgrace my ancestors?—Think of that, David—think what it

would do to disgrace my ancestors!

Title #5, Northumberland: Northumberland is the most northern of the
English counties. Located on the east coast just off the North Sea, its
northern boundary marks the limit of English speech in that direction.
Beyond the Cheviot Hills and the river Tweed, the braw sounds of
Lowland Scots begin. As close as they are, however, there is little mix
between the two dialects.

The speaker in this sequence presents the key sounds of the region as
uttered in everyday speech by the majority of the people in the area. As a
vocal pattern, it is halfway between a dialect that is expressive of an
old-time speech and the vocal accents of a younger person who has been
exposed to the influence of Standard English speech.

Immediately apparent is the key vowel that is so characteristic of all
North-Country speech, the [u] of *by gum* as heard previously in "The
Rivals." Here it is sounded in *sons* and repeated in *took their sons*. The
presence of the broad *a* [ɑ] in *family* and *had* lends distinction; it suggests
an unlikely connection with the broad *a* of Highland Scots, where that
key sound gets heavy use. The elongation of the vowel [eː], as heard in

days, is also to be noted. Not to be missed further along in the transcript is the fine North-Country diphthong in *boats.* Obviously, the speaker is referring to ship models as he talks.

The Pilot

. . . Each family had its own corbell, and if you hadn't a corbell in—in the—in the family, it meant that your sons couldn't be apprenticed to his father. Because it was in the corbells that these young boys served their times to be pilots, or apprentice pilots. On fine days when the vessels, when the corbells could get to sea, the father, and the uncle and the rest of the relatives of the family took their sons away with them . . .

This is a model of a pilot's corbell. You see it's got a very deep stern and a very short after-end. They're about 17 feet long, these vessels, and when they went away to look for ships down at Camberra, when they pick the ship up, they were towed back home by the apprentice in the boat. These boats were moved either by sail or by oars. They had three oars, but you had to be very, very careful you didn't give them too much sail or they'd turn over.

Title #6, Lake District (Westmoreland): This transcript was taped in The Gingerbread Shop,[4] located on the main street of the little town of Grasmere, which is in the middle of England's popular Lake District.

The tape for this title has to be gauged as moderate in dialectal strength. Although the overall impression is quite marked, there are fewer than usual key sounds to be noted. Among them is the North-Country [u] vowel, heard in *money* and in *some.* Then there is an indication of the pervasive middle-class diphthong [aɪ] in the words *eighty-eight.* Interestingly enough, there is a typical Irish key sound of an elongated *o* [o:] in the word *sold.* There is also a tendency to elongate other key sounds, as in the vowel [e:] in *gave.*

The rapidity of the speech, which is a personal characteristic and not a dialectal distinction, makes analysis somewhat difficult. As with some titles in this book, both the transcript and the tape are necessary in order to get a clear or semiclear understanding of the speech.

[4] The product being baked and sold was not the gingerbread cookie or cake that we know. It was, instead, an English toffy-like confection, nicely spiced and very tasty.

The Gingerbread Lady

[Well, it was said that the husband used to drink, and she'd] no money, and she worked, worked in one of the big houses, and there was a Frenchman there who gave [her] this recipe. He told her—told her to keep it in her head, tell nobody, that some day it may make her a few shillings, he said. Well, she started making this gingerbread, and she'd sit outside on a chair, and she'd sell it outside—she'd no children, so when she died in nineteen-hundred-and-four, she was eighty-eight, and she left the recipe to her two nieces.

Well, they, of course—trade got a little bit better, you see—well, then, when they were retired, and they sold the recipe, you see, they sold it, you see. Well, now—to the present owner's aunt. So she always told my son-in-law that he—he could have the first chance if he could raise the money to buy the recipe, not the business, the recipe. It's on a piece of paper locked in the bank. Even my daughter hasn't even seen it, you know that. (*He's the only one!*) He's—he's, well, of course, then of course his aunt who bought the business, who he bought the business off—(*But you know it because you mix the whole thing up.*) Oh, but I couldn't do the mixing. I—I—I—weigh it, and I treat and bake it and cool it and cut it, but I don't know the secret of the recipe. (*He does!*) He does! (*He's the only one!*) And in the bank!

No date in English history is better known than 1066. It was a watershed year; all that was Saxon and now is English was altered because of what took place during a span of days in this one year. In the month of October William the Conqueror crossed the English Channel from Normandy and, landing on the southeast coast of England, fought, defeated, and killed Harold, the Saxon king, in the Battle of Hastings. From that date on William has had the better of it in the history books.

Yet, Harold, some of us feel, deserves a better report than he has had. From the beginning, the Battle of Hastings was an indecisive conflict. Until one crucial moment Harold and his Saxon followers had much the better of the fight. Actually, in the days before that crucial moment Harold had performed a remarkable feat. Even as William was threatening to cross the English Channel to attack England's southeast coast, a prince by the name of Tostig, Harold's half-brother, was landing farther up the shoreline in Yorkshire with an army of Norsemen and Danes. Tostig's purpose, like William's, was to seize the Saxon crown. Harold and his troops, to meet this first threat, moved north by forced marches from London, and at the Battle of Stamford Bridge, against superior numbers, totally defeated Tostig. Then, without pause, with more forced marches, Harold hurried south to meet William on the site of what is now the little town of Battle, just north of Hastings. For most of the day Harold was winning the fight. One crucial error, however, by some of his followers turned victory into defeat.

It is understandable, then, that in Yorkshire the name of Stamford Bridge has some meaning. It was near the site of that bridge, with cars passing in the background, that a local resident, Yorkshire born and raised, talked with me about the battle and the bridge. A slight breeze occasionally registers on the mike.

Title #7, Yorkshire: If 1066 is one of the best-known dates in English history, the distinctive Yorkshire speech is one of the most popular of all the English regional dialects. It has been used extensively in the country's literature; playwrights and actors have been just as active in its use. One only has to hear it spoken to know the reason why, as the tape for "The Bridge" demonstrates. In this case, the donor's key sounds and melodic patterns offer the student an excellent source for study. Although it is not as strong as the dialect heard in "The Rivals," still it is typical of both Yorkshire and England.

Distinctively Yorkshire is the [u] vowel heard throughout the transcript as heard in the words *supposed, just,* and *reproduction.* With this is the North-Country tendency to elongate certain vowels, especially the [e:] in *taken* and *Danes.* Typically middle class (and lower class) is the dropped [ʜ] in *have* and *here* and the softened or elided [ɾ] in *there* and *here,* together with the dropped [ø] in *ing* and the diphthong, or triphthong, [ʌou]. Also apparent, although not in full strength, is a glottal stop [ʔ], which appears several times. Further, as discussed in the Introduction, the pitch inflection on *wouldn't they* in the first sentence sounds just as English as it should.

At one point in the taping the donor spoke of fishing in the North Sea from a small boat, b-oo-aa-t, he pronounced it, repeating the word several times. Unfortunately, the sound of a passing lorry renders that section of the tape unfit for reproduction. However, the enlongated vowel sound of [o:] and [ʌ:], as in *boat* or *coat,* can be heard in quite a few English regional dialects, some as far off as Cornwall and Wales.

The Bridge

. . . They'd have made a bridge there, wouldn't they? You see, they're supposed to have crossed just here, according to that leaflet. They had a, when they had a reproduction, a film—(*Ah, yes.*) you know—(*Un-huh*)—a few years ago, they had the bridge across further down there. . . . The Danes' Well, they're just through there—(*Uh-huh*) eh, where they were supposed to have taken their water, I think. It's a—a fresh-water spring. (Ah, there's a spring there—) It's called the Danes' Well, it just is running a little bit now. (*Ah, I see.*) It's blocked it with roots, I think, tree roots, but. . . .

[There was a question about the use of the river.] No, not a lot, really. There's—a—some big schemes underway for reopening it for navigation, they got it done from, you can get at it from Elvington to Stamford Bridge, now, and they're wanting to open this up as far as it goes, right up to—(*What would they run?*)—Scarborough, somewhere—(—*freight boats, canal boats, or* —)—there used to be, ah, coal barges. There's a—if you go up there and take the first turn left, just before you get to the river again, there's a hill and it's called the Coal Yard Hill, and there's a big, ah, old pit hole on the right-hand side, and it was supposed to be where the coal barges unloaded. (*I see, un-huh. But it's not used for much now.*) No, it's a shame, really, isn't it?

. . . (*Are you Yorkshire born?*) Ah, yes, yes. (*Where, where 'bouts*—) Market Weighton where I was born. That's on the York Hole Road, you know. (*Ah, yes.*) This is the Bridlington Road, and the one—have you been into York? (*Yes, we came through there.*) Where you come out there's a fork, isn't there? (*Yes.*) Just back up here—(*Yes*—) take the right fork, that's the Hole Road, and I was born at Market Weighton. Me father was a blacksmith, in a little village, just up there.

Title #8, Midlands: Central England is industrial England. Stretching from beyond Manchester in the north to below Birmingham in the south are the country's manufacturing towns and cities. Shopkeepers and workers, merchants, managers, and mechanics inhabit these highly urbanized centers.

The resultant composite speech is rich with a mixture of speech patterns that literally have come from all over the country. Dominant, however, as you will hear, are the middle-class (and lower-class) key sounds of the large body of working people.

The voice on the tape belongs to a labor leader who expresses his political point of view in a manner that is typical of the democratic system. The council session was open to all, and the subjects discussed were a matter of public debate. The form of address used by the speaker gives a nice sense of historical continuity.

In spite of strong working-class connections, note that the *g* of *ing* is not dropped, and there is no glottal stop. In addition, the initial *h* of *Housing* comes through clearly, even though the *wh* is not sounded in *Whitehall* and *what*. Outside the council meeting, however, all of these key sounds most likely would be heard in abundance. There is, of course, the pervasive [aɪ] diphthong, heard in *Mayor*, together with the all-British use of [ɔː] and the elided [ɾ], as in *course*, and the [ʌou] of *Housing* and *program*.

City Council

ɔːɾ   aɪə   ʌou   ɔːɾ ə   ʌou   ɾ   aɪ
Lord Mayor, the Housing Finance Act, of course, is going to have its part to play

                    ʌou   eː   ɾ   aɪ   ɔː
in the building program. Because they introduce a very—ah—nice thing called

                                              ɾə   aɪ ɾ ʌou
reckonable and nonreckonable expenditure, and they are going to decide, that is,

aɪ   ʜ   ɔː   ʌɪ   ʌɪ   ʌou
they, the government, Whitehall, the usual people, the people that know everything

       ɾ   ɔː   ʌɪ   →
and are all-seeing, are going to tell us what we can spend by the cost yardstick

and what as of that will be reckonable expenditure. And if it is not reckonable

expenditure, who do you think pays, the rate payer, of course. [meaning the

taxpayer] On top of that, so they're going to pay double rents, and this is why we

said that the Housing Finance Act is a rotten act, a divisive act, and a class-based

act, and we opposed it then and we oppose it now, and when we get a Labor

government next time, we shall throw it out.

Title #9, Midlands (Derbyshire): Located approximately halfway between the industrial cities of Manchester and Birmingham is the manufacturing town of Derby (porcelain and weaving), surrounded by farming country. It is the rural dialect of the shire that is emphasized in the first portion of the following tape. The donor is an English actor-producer who first gives us something of his native Derbyshire speech and then adds other Midland bits of speech from Birmingham and Liverpool. The regional dialects are heard in sharp contrast to his usual Standard English speech.

As you will hear, the principal distinction of a Derbyshire dialect is the inbred and long-established corruption of commonplace words, which is a phenomenon that attracts more attention than the regional pronunciation. For this reason the usual phonetic transcription will not be given at the beginning of the transcript.

For additional source material in written form see D. H. Lawrence's *Lady Chatterly's Lover*. Lawrence himself was born in Derbyshire, and the gamekeeper in the novel reflects Lawrence's intimate knowledge of this dialect.

A Right Wasya

We're in Derby, Derbyshire [and] the accent is really quite strange. There are, sort of influences from medieval times, like they say, "All right, Sorry." *Sorry* is a corruption for *Sirrah,* meaning *friend.* So they use the word *Sorry.* You think everybody is saying they're sorry, but what they mean is friend, is a corruption of *sirrah.*

And they have a saying there that's, "He was a right Wasya." Now a *right Wasya* is somebody who has got a real Derbyshire accent. "He's a right Wasya." "Wasya doin'?" "Wasya goin' to work, youth?" [meaning *lad*] "Wasya goin' to come with us?" "Wasya." "He's a right Wasya," meaning *a right were you.*

[Further word distortions] You know, there'a a guy comes into pub and he says, "Aye up, youth, how you goin'? You goin' to work today, youth?" And he'd ask you for a cigarette like, and he'd say, "Hast any on you got a cigarette on you?" Which means, "Have any of you got a cigarette, on you?" . . . They always say, "I donna wanna go." Or "You shouldna do it," instead of "I don't want to go." "You shouldn't do it." And you can place men by their villages. "What are you doing?" "Where are you about?" "What are you doing?" "Where you?" "Doon, na," they say. *Doona* and *coona* for couldn't, you see—*doona* and *couldna. Doona, wanna, shouldna,* I *wanna—*

They [also] say: "Derbyshire born and Derbyshire bred, strong in the arm, and thick in the head."

[*And the Birmingham dialect?*] Well, in Birmingham they talk like this, you know, it's a very rounded sort of accent. I spent quite some time in Birmingham, so going around, you know, I started to pick it up. I started speaking like they do down there. But it's very interesting, you know, because within Birmingham itself there are three or four different accents, and you can get into one area, like in Ladypool, I remember one morning I was going down the road and this guy came along and I said to him, "Where are we?" He said, "You're in Ladypool Road." I said, "Well, how do I get down to St. Mary's School?" And he said, "You go down here, turn left, you find yourself (?) in Ladypool Road." I couldn't understand a word he was saying.

[*And the Liverpool—Liverpuddlian—dialect?*] Well, the difference between Liverpool and Birmingham is that Liverpool is more back in the throat. They talk like the Beatles, you know, John, Paul, and Ringo and Bert [George], and they say things like "The Mersey" for the river, "the river Mersey," and it's more back in the throat. Then in the Birmingham we chanced to be more forward and rounded, is Birmingham, it's rounded. Liverpool, it's a bit tighter, you know. They talk like, "that Wack." "Wacker, how are you going today, Whacker?" It's quite different.

Title #10, Suffolk: On a quiet Sunday morning in a picturesque little village that time seems to have passed by, a casual question of a stalwart resident introduced us to the next donor's voice that you will hear. It introduced us also to the wool town of Lavenham in the county of Suffolk, England. Inhabited by immigrant Flemish weavers in the thirteenth century, the place remains today much as it was then, albeit word around the tourist trade may alter this condition very shortly.

In the first half of the seventeenth century the country of Suffolk, and especially the area around Lavenham, located north and east of London, was strongly Puritan, both religiously and politically. Cromwell and the Commonwealth drew heavily on the area for support. It was from there that most of the membership of the Massachusetts Bay Colony was recruited. The leader of that committed and disciplined band, the Elder John Winthrop, owned property in and around the village. However, whatever influence the religious character of Puritan speech had, with its biblical emphasis on pronouns and other forms of address, has long been lost among the key sounds of the county's dialect.

Although it is not at all extreme, as compared with some of the older forms of regional speech, the Suffolk dialect is still distinctive, even though it shares many vowel, diphthong, and consonant pronunciations with its neighbors. The familiar [aɪ] and [ʌou] diphthongs, the elongated [ɔ:,ɜ:] and [ɛ:] vowels, and the elided [ɽ] can be recognized immediately. Incidentally, the unusual pronunciation of the word *beauty* seems to be the speaker's own idiosyncracy and, as far as I know, is not common to the area.

Constable and Bellringer

(*Is this your native village?*) No. I am a Suffolk man. I originate from the most easterly point of East Anglia, which is a place called Lowestoft, which is still in the county of Suffolk. That is—ah—seventy miles from here, but it's still the county of Suffolk, and I am still living in the county of Suffolk. I've been living in Lavenham now as the local police officer for nearly ten years. . . .   →

[*Would you tell us something about this unique and very lovely village of Lavenham?*] Well, obviously, you've only got to see it, and once you see it, you can—the beauty of it immediately strikes you. Of course, with the beauty is the age of the place. We all know that this—ah—when the Flemish weavers first came to this country and started—they started up the wool industry in this country, and they had their own weaving looms in their own houses . . .

And of course, your church—well, that's considered one of the finest parish churches in this country. Again, it stands in a commanding position. It's got a facina—fabulous tower. The tower is 142 feet high, and it has a—ah—ring of eight bells, and the tenor bell is considered to be the finest tuned tenor bell in the world, and they've never been able to cast another one quite so good. . .

[The talk switched to bell ringing.] (*How many men in your group? How many ringers?*) Well, we need—we need eight to ring the whole peal. Eight ringers, it's called, and the correct name for it is camponology, but it is more commonly known as change ringing. What, briefly, what happens is you have eight bells and you start, when you start ringing you ring them round, 1-2-3-4-5-6-7-8. You do this for half a dozen times, until you get a nice beat, and a nice even beat, and then when the conductor shouts out the method you are going to ring, he shouts out, and then the bells then go into the changes.

From then on, it's a permutation of eight. We never repeat—repeat the same eight bells twice until they come right back round to (*Oh, yes*) 1-2-3-4-5-6-7-8. What we normally do, is we ring off and on for about 40 to 45 minutes prior to the service. This—this dates back to the old days where you called the people to worship. The bells ringing from the church called the people to worship.

Title #11, Kent: It is said by some historians that the original speech of London came up from the southeast county of Kent and that it was the language of Chaucer and Spenser. MacKenzie MacBride says in London Dialects (1910):

> The London dialect is really, especially on the south side of the Thames, a perfectly legitimate and recognizable child of the old Kentish tongue to which we owe our earliest written literature . . . (it was) the tongue of the first written English, of the first English Church, of the first English scholars, and the first English Schools.

Certainly, some of the key sounds heard today in the regional dialect indicate that they might have been the antecedents of the speech south of the Thames that we call Cockney.

The script for "The Tile Man" came as a result of a sound heard outside the second-story window of an old inn in Kent. As I was leaning out of the gabled casement, I saw a man checking the tiles on the roof. After we greeted one another and spoke a few sentences I reached for a microphone. By holding on to the window frame with one hand and leaning far out, I was able to tape the following conversation.

The speaker was local, born and raised in the area, and traveled little outside it. Moreover, untroubled by the sight of a microphone, he was obligingly voluble in response to my questions. Some of his key sounds indicate that the Kentish dialect might well have been the original of London's Cockney: the [aɪ] of *rine* for *rain*, together with the unmistakable glottal stop, the dropped [h], and several of the other sounds often heard on the preceding tapes. Interestingly enough, his pronunciation of *tiles* is identical with the Irish sounding of the same word, although no identifiable connection can be made between the two.

The sound of wind on the mike, as well as that of birds and cars, intrude on the tape. Also, because of the donor's fast delivery, there is not a clear cut-off of sound where portions of the original tape have been deleted in the editing.

The Tile Man

. . . These tiles—(*yes*)—they are really—yeah, yeah, they're all right. They got a

solid base, some of them are not, but these are pretty solid, you know, but in

general they are brittle. . . . (*How old are these, do you think?*) Oh, these? I don't

know—a couple of hundred years. (*Right here?*) Oh, these tiles probably are,

yes—yes—yeah, they've just been rebedded in because they're rebedded in

concrete. Most of 'em put in, you know, the old tiles put in plaster, just sand and

lime. . . . [*And you can walk on them, they won't break?*] Yeah, they're all right. You

put a ladder up so that they are on the tile all the way. But if you happen to put the

ladder so that it just rests on two—two tiles, they split in the middle. (*Yeah*) But if

you put the ladder so that they're right [h?] up level with the—the weight evenly

distributed on the tiles, this is, you know, what I think [fink?] anyway.

(*All these houses here, are they—*) Yeah, most of these houses are the old,

these are the old tiles, most of these old tiles—ah, you can see the modern tiles

because, you know, they're straight, they're square. The old ones are all bowed,

you know, jagged edges, ah—they are all local quality . . .

But, ah, you know, I doubt if you can see it from here—no, you can't, but there's

a big house up on the hill, at Minton, which used to be called Morris House, and

that house used to, you know, that's where the sort of Lord of Kent lived. (*Oh yes.*)

And he sort of owned everything he could see . . .

[I interposed a question about the weight of the tiles.] Some of these old roofs

have got some terrific weight on them, especially these sort of gaters [gables?]

and that, because some of them, they sort of go right down to the ground, almost.

(*Yes.*) And to the top is most two and three stories up, straight out. They're

thousands and thousands of tiles on some of these roofs.

Title #12, Dorset: It is not often, when one is on a worldwide search for
material for a resource book, that a primary source that one is seeking
presents itself, unbidden and unannounced, at the doorstep. I was
standing at the foot of our steps waiting for the mail carrier when a small
car stopped and a young man leaned out to ask a question. I responded
by asking one myself: "What part of England are you from?" (I was too
cautious to name a region.) "Bournemouth, in Dorset," he replied.

It required only an explanation of my request to get this young man
and his companion to come into my study in front of a microphone. They
talked for over a half-hour and were eager to tell of their experiences in
the United States—prime material that unfortunately had to be sharply
cut in order to squeeze it into an already timed and edited master tape.

The two young men were ingeniously touring the United States by
driving cars to be delivered across the country and by hitchhiking. They
had already moved from New York through the Border States, Texas, and
the Southwest to California. Their return to the East would be by the
northern route.

Their dialect, middle-class and regional, is interesting for several
reasons. First, the long [ɔː], as in *ought, all,* and *law,* is as strong as that
of any speaker of Standard English. Listen for it in *Bournemouth* and *New
York.* Next, the ubiquitous [aɪ] diphthong, which has been so pronounced
on most of the tapes heard so far (the one that changes *make* to *mike*), is
just barely suggested when it is used. It could be, as sometimes happens,
that the two young men, who obviously have sharp ears, were already
making a partial adaptation to the pronunciations they were hearing
around them—a not unusual circumstance for many travelers—and were
modifying what could be an attention getting sound. Both of them used
[i] rather than [ɪ] when they were pronouncing *been,* making [bin], a
usage that is not nearly as prevalent as it used to be. Also, there is the
glottal stop, which is not as strongly sounded as it would be in
full-strength Cockney but is unmistakably there nonetheless. The *r* is
pronounced and not elided or dropped, but not with the strength an
old-timer from Somerset would use.

The Bournemouth Lads

         ' bɔːɟnməθ   ʌou   v
I'm from Bournemouth in England. . . . Well, I came over with a friend, and

   i   ʌou
we've been here about three weeks. We're—our idea was to see the States and to

ɔ: ɔ:t ɒ   ʌou
see as many nice spots as we can. We flew to New York about three weeks ago,

         i   aɪ(?)
and we've been here in California for about two days now.

                                                                              i
[Their reactions to hitchhiking across country—great!] Temperatures have been

        ɔ: ʌou   i   ʌou
really hot, so far, I'd like to say. But the people have been, so far, absolutely

ɑ ɑ   ʔ   ʌou
fantastic, everybody that's picked us up on the highway—we've had no trouble

              ɔ: →
hitching at all, and we've met some really nice people. . . . We stayed in

Albuquerque for about four days with this guy Hugh, and he was really a fantastic

guy. He let us stay at his home, he cooked for us, and he showed us all around the

town.

[As to space] The distances are just fantastic, incredible, because we just

seem to travel on the road all the time, you know. We've been traveling for three

weeks and most of the time we've been on the road and we've only just reached

California from New York.

[The second lad] I'm from Bournemouth in England. It's a very, very sunny

seaside resort. We get a lot of holiday makers there in the summer. It's on the

south coast. It's about a hundred miles from London—it's right down on the south

coast, and I've lived there all my life. . . . I'm going into journalism in September

when I go home, at Portsmouth College to do a journalism course, and that lasts

for a year. [*And what will you study?*] English literature, practical journalism,

law—when I get out of college, I, I hope to go on a local paper. And eventually,

you know, run my own paper, as editor.

Title #13, Somerset: There are rewarding reasons for going to the city of
Bath For one, the Romans, during their occupation of Britain, developed
in spectacular fashion the thermal springs that sent up thousands of
gallons of steaming mineral water each day. As a result, from then until
now the place has been favored as a health resort or spa where people
with all manner of afflictions have come to "take the waters."
    In the seventeenth century, as a result of the entrepreneurial abilities
of Beau Nash, Bath became *the* social center of the country where the *beau*

monde of society came, not only for the waters, but to frequent the gaming and assembly rooms as well. Restraint (law and order) and profligacy (huge sums won and lost at the tables) existed, Monte Carlo-like, side by side.

Bath is located in the northeast section of Somerset county. Its regional dialect, heard in the following tape in modified form, features a unique pronunciation of one key sound. In this area and in some other parts of southwest England as well, the *r*, so consistently elided, softened, or single-tapped in all other places, is here treated very like its overseas cousin in the American Midwest. It is a muscular *r*, enunciated with a hardness that would do credit to any old-timer from the state of Nebraska. The late Robert Newton featured the sound in many of his movie roles; he can still be heard on reruns.

Interesting because of their absence in this dialect are several of the standard key sounds that have been heard on tape after tape, for example, the *so don't go* diphthong [ʌou], the [aɪ] of *rine*, and the [ɔː] of *all*. It is interesting also that although this particular example of the dialect makes a marked impression on the ear, it does not require a heavy notation of phonetic symbols, indicating subtle rather than broad differences. The glottal stop [ʔ], a dropped *h* [ʮ], a *d* for the voiced *th* [ð], and a hint of [ʌoɪ] in *right* and *like* are off-and-on features.

The speaker, an assistant hotel manager, was taped on the landing of a back stairs. He was born and raised in Bath.

The City of Bath

[*If you have lived here all your life, what are your feelings about the place?*] Oh, it's the best city in the country. (*Oh, it is? What makes it so?*) Well, reflecting it's got such a long history, goes right back to pre-Roman times, ah, if you like you can see the Roman baths, the heated ones, naturally of course, the one—the only two in the country, I think, and it stretches back to there. But the main history would be, ah, the Beau Nash era, the 1700s, the—

   (*Who was Beau Nash? What did he do?*) He was the original sort of entertainments officer that sold the city to the country. Originally it was, ah, isolated, as it were, in the 1700s, before the cultures sort of mixed up one another—London, Birmingham. It was sort of isolated, where they came for treatment, for gouts, and various things like that. Years ago that's how they all suffered from gout and scurvy and all those sort of thing, because, (a) they—they

never washed, and (b) they just didn't eat the right food, and he sold as a city and

then—once he got them here, he made a social center for gambling, and all things

like that . . .

And there's a lot of history behind it because Pitt and a few of the other

architects, they designed the city so it would not be in blocks, and so as you

wouldn't see streets. As you came up you see a curved rank of houses, and you

got into the Circus. You look along again and you see another houses offset,

everything is built to, well, you can say this is the first planned city as such.

Title #14, Lower Cotswolds: **This conversation with a stone mason was taped by a country roadside (passing cars will be heard) as he paused in his work on one of the fine old stone walls that are so typical of Somerset and The Cotswolds.**

Here, as in the previous tape, the hard *r* is heard, together with the other key sounds already noted, except that there is no glottal stop. Additionally, there is an especially fine sound, best heard on the word *now* [ɛno]. It is repeated several times throughout the transcript.

A Hard Old Life

>   ř ɛ   ř æ: ʌou   ʌou   ʌou
> . . . Every hill is a different class of stone, you know—you know, different

>   ř   ř   ɸ
> colors and different textures, and—a—this is—a—just ordinary dry-walling

>   æ   ʌoɪ
> stuff—(*Now*—)—'tisn't, 'tisn't anything special. You build dry walls with anything.

>   ʌou   æ: ʌou   ř
> You know, no—no special class of stone. It isn't dressed or anything, merely as

> u   ř   ʁ   ř
> dug. (*Now*—) This is just a repair job. I've got a bit of stuff in here just to repair it,

>   ʌɪ →
> you see.

(*Now, how long, how long—Most of these walls that we see along here, how old*

are they?) Well, there's one over on the other road, and the men, there's men

around about 70, getting on towards 80, and they remember it being built in 1908

(*Ah, yes.*), and it's just beginning to get out of shape now. But it's due to the trees,

you know, and the trees grow and the roots shake it, you know (*Oh, yes.*), they,

they shake it. I should think you give them about 80 to 100 years, that's—(*Well,*

that's pretty good value, isn't it?) Yes, it is, yes. But, well, this stuff, years ago the

men out in the fields they used to go round these walls and keep them up together,

but now, but they start disintegrating, nobody does anything, no one does anything

to them, you know. (*Ah, yes—just let it go.*) Yes—yes.

(*Now, is this your trade? I mean, you are a stone mason?*) Oh, yes—and when I

started 50 years ago, this was the only material you had to build with. But it's a

hard old life.

WALES

The speech of many Welsh persons is indistinguishable from that of many English persons, and the number is increasing, caused by those same factors that are operating every where else in the world today: education, the media, and mobility. Such people are not the focus of our attention.

In the speech of those who still use the Welsh dialect, three things are immediately noticeable:

1. A change of emphasis that stresses a second rather than a first syllable. Listen for the words *Go'wer* and *sing'ing* in the first transcript. This effect is also heard in the pronunciation of proper names, for example, *Mor'gan* and *Grif'fid* (Griffith).

2. The presence of the Welsh lilt, a melodic inflection that in phrase or sentence endings keeps the pitch up when ordinarily it would drop down. Sometimes the effect is subtle, and sometimes it is broad. Again, the word *Go'wer* serves as an illustration. This distinctive feature derives from the use of Gaelic, the national language, which is still taught in the schools and used in conversation, especially in North Wales. Its increased use is strongly advocated by the Welsh Nationalist Party.

3. The absence of those key sounds that have been heard in such abundance throughout the rest of the country, for example, the broad *a* [ɑ], the *so don't go* [ʌoʊ] diphthong, or the other diphthong [aɪ], which is heard when *make* becomes *mike*, and the slurred or dropped *r*. The result of this is that the pronunciation of vowels, diphthongs, and consonants are less noticeably different to American ears than are the key sounds that give distinction to Standard English and middle-class British speech. Consequently, the usual phonetic transcriptions are not given in this series.

A unique feature of Welsh speech is the pronunciation of the double *l—ll* [l̥]—as heard in proper and place names. This particular phoneme, not used elsewhere, is effected when the tip of the tongue, touching the ridge of the upper gum so as to close off the air, causes the air to escape over the sides of the tongue in both directions with a very slight hissing sound. The result is almost an *f*. Examples of this are *Lloyd, Llewellyn, (Fluellen* in *Henry V*), and *Llandudno.*

Title #15, South Wales: The donor of the following selection, a civil engineer, offers a Welsh dialect that also features some typically English sounds, notably those short sentence endings such as *isn't it* and *but there it is.*

The Singing

Well, I'm from Swansea. (*Is that north or south Wales?*) South Wales. (*That is your native city?*) That is my native town, yes. I was born and brought up, you know—my family, of course, all worked underground. (*That means in the mines?*) Yes, in the mines, but near the mines, well, there is a marvelous, ah, sea place, Gower, we call it, Gower Peninsula, ah, really marvelous. You can get some beautiful countryside plus the sea, completely unspoiled. (*Ah, so it is more of a vacation, a holiday spot?*) Well, yes, it is, but you see we don't, they don't encourage people to come there, I don't know why, but they don't want to commercialize it . . .

(*What about the Welsh customs, the old native Welsh customs, are they dying out?*) I'm afraid so, yes, most of them are. The language is dying a lot, you know. It's a pity, but there we are—television and—(*And is the singing dying out?*) Oh, no, that'll never die out—no, no, no. Yes, I know that the Welsh will always be very, very keen, singing, because it's in them, isn't it? You know, it's a, well, we are, we're born with it, as it were. We can't explain it, but there it is.

Title #16, Central Wales: The Welsh have a way of identifying a person by his or her occupation, using the first name but dropping the second or family name in favor of whatever it is the person does. Two donors, both from the middle part of the country, provide us with illustrations. Note how both of them use the Welsh lilt as well as the altered stress; they use more of the first than the second, however.

Names

[*Tell me how names are assigned in the Welsh.*] Oh, I'd be happy to. Ah, for instance, we would call the minister, whose name was Mr. Jones, we'd call him Mr. Jones, the Cloth. And then we had, ah, Johnny, the Sweep—he used to come around and sweep the chimneys for us, ah, with his brushes, and it would make a

terrible mess until the, ah, later on in the years that they would bring a vacuum

cleaner to vacuum up all the soot up on the hearth. Then we had on the village, my

mother used to have our shoes repaired by a, a cobbler, and his name was Islwyn,

the Cobbler. (What was his first name?) Islwyn—it's spelled I-s-l-w-y-n, Islwyn, the

Cobbler.

[*Would you continue with the names?*] Oh, yes. We had John, the Shoe, he's the

local cobbler. Willie the Cop—but that's not a policeman, that's a cooperative

store, every village has a cooperative store, so we call him Willie the Cop. And

then we have Dai Champion. Now, Dai was the flyweight champion of Wales for

many years, and of course we don't call him Dai, the Boxer, we call him Dai

Champion, because he was a champion. Tom, the Paper, he runs our paper shop

on our street.

[He speaks of another character.] . . . a coal miner and an ironworker in a

place called Rumney, Wales, and his name was William Davis, William, the

Leader, because he used to conduct all the various choirs and choral groups in

the Rumney Valley, so they called him Billy, the Leader. But his family called him

Willie Dumplin' because when he was a little boy and as he was growing up he

loved to have Welsh broth with dumplin's, big, suety, meaty dumplin's in there,

and then followed by apple dumplin's—that's an apple with the suet around it, see,

and so they called him, Willie Dumplin'.

IRELAND

There is a melody in the vowels and diphthongs; there is beauty in the phrases; and some of the consonants have a unique sound—all of which makes an Irish dialect as interesting and delightful as any going *a'tall, a'tall.*

As for a discussion of the speech itself, the key sounds are treated in full in my first volume, *Stage Dialects,* with a special emphasis given to the idiom of Sean O'Casey. To that coverage I have added here a dialectal tour of the country, beginning with the regional speech of the south (Cork) and moving through the west and into the north before returning back to the capital of Dublin.

Although Ireland is a full-fledged member of the English-speaking group of the British Isles, one of the first things to be noted about the Irish dialect is the complete absence of several of the key sounds that characterize upper-, middle- and lower-class speech in England, none of which can be heard in Ireland unless the individual Irish person has Anglicized his or her own speech.

True to their proud and fiercely independent character, and Irish have their own key sounds, and on them the distinctive nature of their speech relies, that is, a major use of the [ɑ] as sounded in our accompanying phonetic transcription. It is heard also in a broad assortment of words, such as *odd, army, heart, all, ought, jaw, other, up, half, man,* and *rather,* to list a few. Also, there is a characteristic diphthong, or triphthong, [ʌoɪ], which is heard again and again, making melodic such words as *Mike, fine, night,* and *time.* Then there is the [ʌou] of *out, town,* and *now.* In addition, several vowels [i, e, æ, u, o] are elongated [ː]. Further, the [ř] is hard and fully sounded, as in *Ireland,* and the [g] of *ing* is often dropped, so that *running* becomes *runnin'.* Then, in Dublin, a [d] can replace the *th* [ð] of *these, those,* and *other,* making *dese, dose,* and *de odder.* There are also, many colloquialisms, some of which are heard at the beginning of the tapes.

Title #17, South, West, North, and Central: The donor of the following tape, born in Dublin, is a fine Irish actor who, besides being capable of multiple roles, is a tour de force performer of anything by Brendan Behan. Now working in Hollywood, he has covered much of Canada and the United States in his playing. The attractiveness of his delivery and the versatility of his speech will be immediately apparent.

A Dialect Tour

[The question was asked: What sounds would I hear if I took a tour of Ireland from the south through the west and into the north before returning back to Dublin?]

Well, you know, if you, if you, ah, the first place you'll stop in when you leave

America is County Cork. You arrive in the, in the Cove of Cork—down in *Cobh,*

C-o-b-h, it's called Cove, there's no *v* in the Irish language, so there's only

18 letters in the Irish language—there's no *v*'s, and there's no *j*'s,

and there's no *q*'s—and the Cork people, of course, they're like Cork

itself, they wander up and down—Cork is full of hills, and the Ir—the Cork, the

Corkonians talk up and down, they wander around: "Are you from Cork?" "Bedad I

am." "Do you eat potatoes?" "Bedad I do." "Skins and all?" "Bedad I do." [and]

"Ah, where are you going with no bell on your bike?" They are, they are the singingest—it's the singingest accent in Ireland, is the Cork one, because,

because they are all tenors down there.

So then as you leave Cork and you work your way up through County Clare,

and you sort of hit County Galway, then you find that the accents roll out like the

fog, and if you, if you are familiar with Siobhan McKenna, that way it is, the

beautiful, it's a beautiful west of Ireland fog. Now, Siobhan, she was born in Belfast

but she was raised over in the *Gaeltacht,* which is where they speak nothing but

Gaelic.

And of course then you go from Galway up into County Sligo—now it's not

Sligo, it's *Shligo.* But as you leave Galway and you head up toward County

Donegal, it's getting a little more Scottish, and as you leave Donegal and you

come down into Antrim is where the Belfast people take over, and what the Belfast

people—it's rather clipped because it comes from Glasgow, because the, the

Scottish, ah, influence there when all the Scottish people came over and took over

the land there to propagate the faith for a, for a Queen Victoria.[5] And it's rather

clipped and rather, rather, rather sharp.

But a, when you leave, when you leave Belfast and County Derry, now it's not

Londonderry, it's Derry—you leave Derry and then you, you'll start heading down

towards Dublin. And of course then the Dublin accent, it starts to broaden out a

little bit. And they never say—they don't know where to put their *h*'s in Dublin,

because they say *dis, dat, dese* and *dose* and *dem* and *de odders.* And a, a

Dubliner will give you three different accents, because if you leave the center of

Dublin, and that's the way they talk in the center of Dublin, you slowly move out to

Rathgal, which is rather elegant. And of course we, we Dubliners used to say,

[5] This process first began after William III defeated the Irish at the Battle of the
Boyne, July 1, 1690.

"Thank heaven we are living in Rathgal, even though we cannot afford to buy a car."

Now, then, you'll get the middle class who are halfway between the Dublin thing and the Rathgal thing, which is all very nice. And then when you come to America, you mix the whole up together, and then you end up what I am arrived at.

Title #18, Dublin: The donor of this selection tells of the days when she first came from her home to the capital city of Dublin. She talks about the town and imitates some of its people.

Reminiscences

. . . So then I got in with the horse racing, and I used to go out to the Curragh and bet me few bob on the horses and—(*Did you have any luck?*)—I didn't have too much, no, it was not so good, not so good, not so good. But I loved everything except the weather. As they said one time, they said Ireland would be a great country if you could put a roof on it. And the, the rain and, and of course I was there in 1946 and at that time there was no heat, you know. They had no coal, and of course the turf wouldn't warm anything in a, in a furnace. It was all right if you could dry it out in a fireplace, but as they said, there was the man who ran into the back of a turf lorry and was drowned. So, anyway that didn't do you much good.

. . . [Now] I want to tell you about a little street just back of Nelson's Pillar called Mary Street. Now that's where you have the pushcarts, and you have the lovely Dublin ladies there who sell apples and oranges and things, and they say, "Tuppence each the apples and oranges!" and they say also if they get into a fight—they'd have a big fight and a row with each other, and they'll be pulling each other's hair out, and one says, "Ah, go on you!" and other one says, "What are you talking about, you old bag!'' And the other one says, ''Ah, you have your

glue!''

. . . [An excerpt from a play written around the turn of the century.] It's a bad

night, and a wild night, and isn't it a long while I am sitting here at the foot of the

back hills, sitting up here boiling food for himself, and food for the brood sow, and

baking a cake when the night falls? Isn't it a long while I am sitting here in the

winter and the summer, and the fine spring, with the young growing behind me

and the old passing, saying to myself one time, to look on Mary Brien who wasn't

that height and I a fine girl growing up, and there she is now with two children, and

another coming on her in three months or four.

SCOTLAND

Experience has demonstrated that all forms of Scottish speech, from the capital Edinburgh as well as from the various regions, are among the most difficult to master in an authentic manner of all dialects anywhere in the world, but they are worth the time and effort spent on mastering them because of the distinctive and delightful speech that results.

Much of the difficulty is because new muscular movements of a dextrous nature must replace established and easier patterns of articulation. Here are examples:

1. The Scots burr [rʳ], which is produced by tapping or trilling with the front of the tongue with all the flexibility of an opera singer. Check this in Title #19.

2. The same action is used to make another distinctive sound, which is *eh* [ɛ] with a tapped or trilled [rʳ] added, changing, for example, the word *perfect* to *pairfect*.

3. The [u], as in *pool*, is muscularly altered by lips, tongue, and jaw to a French-like [y], as in the French word *une*, so that *foot* [fʊt] has the softer, fuller sound of *fut* [fyt].

4. The German-like [x] is a sound that only the Scots use and is not heard elsewhere in the British Isles. It is necessary for a correct pronunciation of *loch* [lɔx] (lake) or the often used exclamation *ach!* [ɔx].

5. Another unusual sound is the aspirated [ç] of *bright* ['brʳɪçt] or *night* ['nɪçt].

6. The glottal stop [ʔ] is used in such commonplace words as *got* [gɔʔ] or *better* ['bɛʔɛʳ].

In addition, there are several vowel substitutions to master that change the sound of many common words:

1. [ɪ] to [ɛ]—*bit* [bɪt] becomes *bet* [bɛt]
2. [e] to [æ]—*take* [tɛk] becomes *tak* [tæk]
3. [ɛ] to [i]—this is an older Scottish pronunciation that changes *head* [hɛd] to *heed* [hid].

Title #19, Stirling: The following two short pieces give an excellent demonstration of several distinctive key sounds in the Scottish dialect. The donor, born in Scotland, here contrasts the Standard English of her now usual speech with the remembered accents of her youth.

The Owl

. . . and this was what actually happened in a school many years ago. A child

was asked to give a definition of an owl, so he replied, "An owl is an animal with a

cock's head and a chicken's body, and it sits all night in a bush and cries

hooooo."

. . . I remember one girl my mother overheard in a hotel in Glasgow. This girl

was beautifully turned out and she might have been anybody, and then a young

man sat down beside her, and she turned to him and she said, "I would have

waited for you for hours, but what I didn't want was the others to know that I was

waiting for you."

Title #20, Glasgow: The words of the speaker in the following tape are
excerpted from comments made in a public discussion of housing
conditions in the city of Glasgow. The word flow contains a full catalogue
of the key sounds of Glaswegian speech. Present, but not as strongly
evident as it might be, is the distinctive melodic pattern that is
characteristic of even casual Glaswegian talk. It is an indeterminate pitch
inflection at the ends of phrases and sentences that stays up rather than
falls in the normal manner. Although this particular practice can be heard
in regions other than Glasgow, nowhere else is it used quite as
distinctively.

Glasgow Housing

. . . I think, Sir Robert, to some extent that this has been over emphasized, the

question of rehabilitation existing in houses, the old houses. I've heard the word

used twice tonight as the casualties in relation to human, uh, people, and also the

properties that we've been talking about. Now, one must accept, surely, that some

of the properties that you've mentioned were really casualties when they were

built, you see. And it's a double casualty sometimes to try and preserve something

which should never have been there in the first place.

It is a fact that some of the people who are forced to leave Council houses, which are relatively low, low rents by almost any standards, are going into Shelter houses at double the rents. That's some of the problem. So it's not a case simply of bringing a volunteer organization in, although they play a very useful part, but it's not simply a case of bringing them in to save these people. Other what should be done via other social agencies so that they don't get into arrears in the first place, because they are leaving a very up-to-date house because of these arrears and going into a, almost a substandard house by comparison.

Title #21, Glasgow: Another Glaswegian reads this old Scots' song. Some of the words belong more to yesterday than to today, but then so does much of Scotland's best literature. Listen to the unique pronunciation of [ç] in *bright, light, night,* and *right.* Note also the typically Glaswegian pitch pattern on the lines ending with "butt an' ben" and "you ken."

Doch an' Dorris

Just a wee doch an' dorris,

Just a wee yin, that's a',

Just a wee doch an' dorris

Before we gang awa'.

There's a wee wifey waitin'

At the wee butt an' ben,

An' if you can say

It's a braw, bright moonlight night,

Then you're a' right, you ken.

(He repeats more slowly)

An' if you can say

It's a braw, bright moonlight night, (the night)

You're a' right, you ken.

Title #22, Wester Ross: The speaker in the following transcript is a petrol station owner who was directing us further into the western Highlands of Scotland. The taping, which was done to help us follow road signs, is noteworthy for the strength of its key sounds, especially the [x], as heard in *Loch* [lɔx], and the French [y], as heard in *Poolewe* [' puly].

Road Directions

(*Start with where we are now.*) Now, you leave the hotel, turn right, follow up the

road till you see the sign for Beauly (*Beauly*), turn right, go over hill, head for Muir

of Ord, through Muir of Ord bear left for Achnesheen. Straight through Achnesheen

up Loch Maree, through Loch Maree into Garloch. From Garloch right round into

Poolewe, Inverewe Gardens—(*What was that last?*) Poolewe, P-o-o-l-e—from

there into Inverewe Gardens. Leave the Gardens, turn left, go right down to, down

Loch Broom right down to Ullapool, and from there right back down back here.

(*Ah, yes.*) Think you can manage that? (*Ah, yes. Thanks very much.*)

Title #23, the Highlands: Many years ago in the "wee" pub attached to Kingshouse, a famous Highland inn located on the windswept edge of Rannoch Moor (just above Glen Coe Pass where the Campbells massacred the MacDonalds), a bonnie lass sang this old "Hieland" song, and the locals at the bar stopped their "clack" to listen and the players at the dart board paused in silent approbation. The spelling in the script is the modern equivalent of the older sounds.

A Bonnie Lass Sings ("The Old Maid's Song")

I have often heard it said, from my father and my mother,

That to go to a wedding is the making of another,

And if that be true, I will go without a bidding,

If I only had an old man to take me to a wedding.

(Refrain:)

Singing, oh, dear me, what will I do,

If I die an old maid in a garret?

I've a younger sister, Kate, and she's both handsome and good-looking,

Scarce sixteen and she had a fellow courting,

Now she's twenty-one with a son and a daughter,

And I am thirty-four and I have not had an offer,

(Refrain:)

I can cook and I can sew, I can make a wee house tidy,

Get up early in the morning and get the breakfast ready,

Do anything at all, it would make my heart so cheery,

If I only had an old man to call me his own dearie,

(Refrain:)

So come tinker or come tailor, or come soldier or come sailor,

Come any man at all who will take me from my father,

Come rich man, come poor man, come wise or come witty,

Come any man at all who will marry me for pity.

(Refrain:)

Title #24, Skye: The speaker in the following tape, a native of the island of Skye, ran a small hotel in a wee town on the northwest coast of Scotland.

The Hotel Keeper

. . . (*Do you like it here?*) Yes, I like it. I feel that if I had been born here, I would have liked it much more, let's put it that way, yes. (*How long is your tourist season?*) Very short in comparison with other places because we're so cut off here. (*Yes.*) I would say about four months, late May to mid-September. (*Then what do you do for the rest of the year? Do you have many visitors?*) No, no, the village is absolutely dead, absolutely dead, yes, yes, yes, very, very quiet.

(*What then do you do? You just live within your portion of—*) Yes, I go visit my son at Macleans, and go and see the children at school, and dismantling, and then after you enter the new year, I begin to mantle up again, get ready for the season, yes, yes, it takes you a little while to get everything dismantled, and then you have to start again. You have a month or two in between, and I go over and see my family and visit, yes, yes. (*I rather imagine you like a rest by that time.*) Oh, yes, you're glad to have a rest, yes, and have a little bit of social life, because you don't have any after the season [opens], no.

Australia and New Zealand

Although Australia and New Zealand are situated half a world away from England and the British Isles, it is logical to list their dialects immediately after those of the mother country. Both of these relatively new nations first came into being as colonies established by the British Empire. The original colonists were immigrants from England, Ireland, Scotland, and Wales. As a consequence, the speech was thoroughly British.

Since the colonists came from the home islands, and there was a plentiful mix of dialects from the many regions, it was only natural that the resultant speech would be a composite of all the original sources. Consequently, certain home island key sounds will be immediately recognizable.

The first of these key sounds is the ubiquitous [aɪ], the diphthong that makes *rine* [raɪn] out of *rain* [ren]. Although this key sound certainly is anathema to the ears of those who use Standard English,[1] yet it seems to be the most commonly spoken syllable in English speech throughout the world. It will be heard in plentiful supply on the tapes ahead.

[1] Standard English itself, in full strength or modified, can be heard in both countries.

Other already familiar key sounds that may be heard in these two dialects are:

1. the broad [ɑ], as in *father:* for example, *after* [ɑftə], *master* [mɑstə], *command* [kə'mɑnd], and *staff* [stɑf]
2. the [ɔː] of *all* [ɔːl], *law* [lɔː], and *awful* [ɔːfəl]
3. the *so don't go* diphthong [ʌou]
4. the dropped or softened [r], as in *there* [ðɛə] and *year* [jɪə]

AUSTRALIA

The first thing to be said about Australian speech is that it has as distinct a character in itself as any in the British Commonwealth. It reflects the origins of the original immigrants, made up in part by the draining of English jails (a fact to which most Australians point with pride) and in part by those venturesome souls who sought the challenge of an undeveloped land and a new way of life. The speech, therefore, is noticeably vigorous and has a charisma, a kind of machismo all its own. As one

Australian said on returning home after spending many years in the United States, listening to the flow of talk in a Sydney bar, "My God, this isn't a dialect—it's an assault!"

And so it might be. To all the sounds of the British Isles, the Australians have added many of their own, and they are both varied and colorful, as the lyrics of *Waltzing Mathilda* bear witness. For example, one of the popular bathing spots in Sydney is a place named Bondi Beach. More than once we heard it called *Bondai Boich* [' bondaɪ ' bʌoɪtʃ]. Then there is the repeated use (strong but not uni-

versal) of the [ɛ] vowel when *yes* [jɛs] is pronounced *yeas* [jɛɪs]. When asked the name of a casual acquaintance, one young man said he did not know, except that he remembered it began with a *poi*, a *p*.

One day in Sydney I pretended to be lost, and in the space of three blocks I asked directions of three individuals. Truthfully, I heard the unmistakable accents of a Glaswegian (a Scot from Glasgow), a Liverpudlian (Liverpool), and a young lad from Belfast, in that order, and not one of their accents was anything less than strong.

Title #1, Sydney: The following transcript came from a much traveled Australian and was taped in a bar in a Spanish parador. The donor was a young, educated man of the managerial class, and his speech is very representative of a wide, middle group. There is no lack of distinguishable key sounds, one of which, the flat front vowel [æ], as in *at*, suggests a Cockney inheritance, for nowhere is its use more pronounced than when a London citizen, born within the sound of Bow Bells, says *town* [tæhn], *now* [næh], and *about* [æ' bæht]. It will be heard on this tape in the word *around* [æ' ræhnd].

The Races

   . . . We have these picnic races in Australia. In other words, it's just a paddock which some grazier puts aside, and they run a few horses around. They do all stupid things like moving the finishing poles, you know, and all those other little—that's, that's really getting off the track. One—one—one small event in a little town called Walgett—we had a grazier, one of the local prominent graziers, by the name of Grey. Boobsey Grey, they called him. Why he got the name Boobsey, I don't know. (*Grazier?*) A grazier—of land, land, sheep, turf. Ah, now Boobsey Grey had a horse that could run a mile and a half, but a couldn't run a mile and three-quarters. The race was over a mile and three-quarters. So they moved the finishing pole to a mile and a half, and his horse won.

Title #2, Queensland: The speaker is a middle-class homemaker. Her dialect is close to average.

The Turtles

[She has just been asked if she has ever been out on the Great Barrier Reef.] Yes, yes, I have done. I had a week there just last November, on Heron Island, which is right on the reef. Beautiful little island, a really beautiful little island. Right—it's a coral atoll, that's what it is. (*Yes.*) . . . Heron is about one and a quarter miles around, that's the size of it, the diameter. Beautiful little island, and it—I was there in November, when the turtles were laying their eggs, (*Ah, yes.*) and after tea—after tea at night we used to go out and walk along the beach, and one night we counted 30 turtles, up making their nests. (*Making their nests? Not laying their eggs?*)—and laying their eggs. They take all night to lay their eggs, then you see—and you go early in the morning and you see them all going back to the water again. (*Leaving the eggs behind?*) They cover them up, they cover their eggs, and then they just leave them, and they're—they're about three weeks before they hatch.

NEW ZEALAND

The speech of New Zealand (as we heard it over a period of more than a month) reflects the social, political, and economic life of the people. There is more of an evenness and a consistency than is usual in most areas. There are no noticeable evidences of great wealth, and there are no marked indications of poverty either, as nearly as we could see in our coverage of most of both North and South Island. A substantial middle class uses the speech that the original settlers brought with them, which is a mixture of dialects from the counties of England, with Cockney, Irish, and Scots thrown in, all made smooth by use through time. Standard English seems to have less influence than might be expected, especially in the speech of national and educational leaders.

As I explained in the Introduction, some of the source material that you will hear in this section is read, not spoken in our usual dialogue form. The transcript of Title #3 is taken from a fisheries pamphlet, fittingly symbolic of an attractive feature of New Zealand life, and the reading was taped in the fourth-form classroom of what we would call a junior high school. The donor voices are those of the teacher and two of the students.

In addition to the key sounds already discussed

in the Australian section, you should note the schoolmaster's pronunciation of 13 (*thir'teen*) [θɜ·'tin] and 14 (*four'teen*) [fo'tin], both of which are typical of a manner that is consistent throughout the mother country and all her former colonies, and that is as noticeable in Standard English as in any of the regional dialects. By chance this singular pronunciation has seldom crept up in any of the transcripts.

Also to be noted is the strength of a flat upper-front vowel when [ɪ] replaces [ɛ], as is heard twice in the word *independent*. Equally strong is the flatness that the second reader, an Australian lad, gives the word *carefully*, in which he changes the vowel [ɛ] into one that is not yet catalogued in the phonetic alphabet. Although there is no relationship whatsoever in those two pronunciations, they have an emphasis that would make any Bronx boy proud. The sound, probably of Cockney origin, is common to both Australia and New Zealand.

Title #3, South Island: Because the first reader's (a student) dialect is stronger than that of the teacher, the phonetic transcription will begin with his reading.

The Fourth Form

. . . I have a mathematics class here, and I'm going to ask some members of the class to come up and read something to you. . . . I should have said that this is a fourth-form class. These boys and girls are about, oh, 13, 14—14 years old, they tell me. Well, now, Bill, you carry on reading, will you?

"If we consider the trout's basic food supply in greater detail, we find that the May fly nymphs, caddis worms and other larvae in their turn are independent, mainly on the microscopic plants which live on the bottom of the stream, and thus these become the primary link in the trout's food chain. If, as so often happens in New Zealand, rivers flood, then the stones of the river bed are overturned, silt is deposited, and many of the insects and plants on which they feed are temporarily destroyed.

[The Australian] . . . "If we carefully examine trout habitats, we find large numbers of trout in the more suitable spawning rivers, or in rivers that are less likely to flood. If we study the distribution of brown trout, we shall find that they do not extend much farther north than Rotorua in the North Island, and that they are also are missing from many of the east coast rivers."

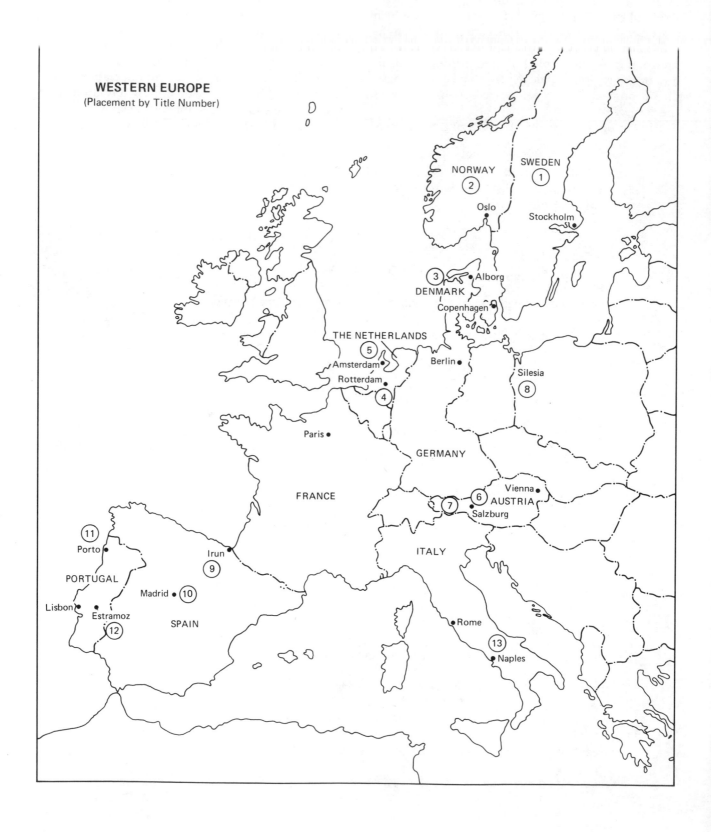

WESTERN EUROPE
(Placement by Title Number)

SWEDEN ①

NORWAY ②

Oslo

Stockholm

③
Ålborg
DENMARK

Copenhagen

THE NETHERLANDS ⑤

Amsterdam
Rotterdam

Berlin

Silesia ⑧

④

Paris

GERMANY

Vienna
⑥ AUSTRIA
⑦ Salzburg

FRANCE

⑪
Porto
Irun
⑨
PORTUGAL
Madrid ⑩

ITALY

Lisbon
Estramoz
⑫
SPAIN

Rome

⑬ Naples

Western Europe

Sweden, Norway, Denmark,
The Netherlands, Austria, Germany,
Spain, Portugal, (and Italy)

Three of the accents of Western Europe—French, Italian, and German—are presented in full in my first book, *Stage Dialects*, and will not be included here.[1]

With four exceptions—Cajun, Jewish, Spanish, and African—all the donors in the first part of this book speak English as a first or a native language; accordingly, their deliveries were recorded as dialectal variations of the one tongue. With only one exception,[2] all the voices yet to be heard belong to donors whose native language is not English. Naturally, the vocal proficiency in the new speech of each of these donors has been determined by the manner and the intensity of his or her study and practice—the process that determines the quality of the resultant accent. Paradox-

ically, the more proficient the manner is and the greater the concentration is on the study of the new language, the poorer the quality of the accent becomes. In contrast, given sufficient clarity to be understood, the poorer the preparation is, the better the accent is likely to be, especially for the dialect student's purposes.

For many Europeans, when economic and social conditions were unsatisfactory and there was little hope for future improvement, individuals who had the will to do so sought to better themselves and their families by moving to the United States. One of the conditions that aggravated their situations in their native lands was a limited education. (Certainly in their schooling the formal study of a foreign language was a luxury beyond their means.)

So these individuals and their families came to the United States or Canada with negligible skills in vocal and written communication in English. Unless they lived in an enclave that was solidly

---

[1] There is one minor exception. The former province of Silesia in old northeast Germany, which has a unique substitution of z for s, is represented in this text.

[2] The donor of "The Man from Minnesota" is an American.

populated by their peers—a situation that has caused their descendants several generations later to speak still with a rich and colorful accent—they were forced daily to increase their expressiveness in the new language on what could only be a haphazard basis. The result was an untutored but attractive speech, which has become a splendid tool of expressiveness for today's actor.

It is not surprising, then, that the large majority of donors in the rest of this book are immigrants who had to acquire English as part of a hit-and-miss learning process, which was an undisciplined by-product of their working and living conditions.

To demonstrate this point, you should listen to the two Hungarian donors. The first voice that you will hear is an immigrant in this country who was taped in the language learning lab where she was earnestly working to acquire proficiency in her new language. She offers a splendid accent for study. The second voice that you will hear had studied English in the course of formal schooling. Consequently, although she is a better communicant, she offers a less distinctive accent for our use.

The United States, as well as Canada (which in the last several decades has had an immigration program considerably heavier than our own), offers a rich field for study to the dialect student, which is often superior to much that is found abroad. The son of a Swedish immigrant, for example, in "The Man From Minnesota," gives us an accent that is much better than anything that can be heard in the land where his father and mother came from, and he is only one of many who will be heard on the tapes ahead.

Of the nine accents covered in this section, six are members of the Indo-European language group, that is, three Scandinavian, one Dutch, one Austrian, and one German. They are Teutonic-based and all have many key sound characteristics in common, which is a beneficial accommodation to the dialect student. We will begin the study of this group with a presentation of the principal elements of sound that pertain to them all.

Here are the key sounds, beginning with those that will receive the greatest use:

1. *v* for *w* or *wh:* *was* becomes *vas* and *which* becomes *vich.* In reversal there will be a few times when *v* becomes *w,* which is hinted at, for example, in the Danish transcript in the pronunciation of *government.*
2. *d* for the voiced *th* [ð], so that *that* becomes *dat.*
3. *t* for the voiceless *th* [θ], in which *thousand* becomes *tousand.*
4. *r,* the most manipulated sound in the whole dialectal lexicon, will be pronounced with the hardness of an American Midwestern *r* in the Swedish transcript and the second of the Dutch transcripts. It will be rolled with the back of the tongue in the first Danish transcript and will receive a treatment that sounds normal to American ears in the first Austrian transcript.
5. [j] This phonetic symbol is sounded as the *y* in *yet.* In the Swedish, the word *just* becomes *yust* and *jiminy* becomes *yiminy.*
6. [ɛʳ] This is the combination of [ɛ], as in *eh,* and the consonant [r], the latter being formed by an action of the back of the tongue, so that *air* [ɛʳ] results. This special formation, heard in the Teutonic parts of Western Europe, is also prevalent in Eastern Europe and Greece. It replaces the English sound *er* [ɜ], as heard in *word, earth,* or *heard.* By chance it is not as noticeable on the tapes ahead as it might, or should, be.
7. Intermittently, an *s* is substituted for a *z,* so that *was* [wɑz] becomes [wɑs].
8. Occasionally a *k* will be added to *ing.*
9. Also, occasionally a *t* might be substituted for a terminal *d,* so that *and* becomes *ant.*

SWEDEN

Title #1: The main strength of the accent in the next transcript comes from its principal attraction, the melodic inflection of a pitch pattern. It is, of course, the characteristic by which the Swedish accent is best known in America. It derives from the mother country's speech, in which the usual inflections so necessary to express attitudes and thoughts are given an extra flourish and can be heard, though not to the extent we expect, in the dialogue of a Swedish film. The Swedish immigrant gives us a much better sound. It is as if in his attempts at speaking the English of his new country, he held onto and increased his tendency to inflect his syllables—an action that might have been further exaggerated for the pleasure of the response it created, and pleasurable it is, as we shall see. A wavy line, ‿, indicates its presence.

The donor, a teacher and an administrator, was president of a Regional Theatre Conference at the time of this taping. Although it is far removed in time and space from the original source of his Swedish accent, he still has it in fluent control, providing us with an excellent transcript.

In addition to the key sounds listed above, two others must be noted:

1. [y] This phonetic symbol, of use in both the German and French as well as the Scotch, Swedish, and Norwegian languages, is formed by rounding the mouth as if sounding the [u] in *too* while pronouncing [i] (*eat*) or [ɪ] (*it*) instead. It will be heard in the words *two* and *school*.

2. The [ʃ], as in *sheep*, replaces the [tʃ], as in *church*. The sound will be heard later in the word *chicken*.

The Man from Minnesota

I just came from Minnesota, and holy gee whillikers how cold it gets up there in the

winter time. They put the—the bells on the horses and they jingle as they go down

through the snow drifts. It's a, it's really kind of thrilling to freeze your nose and

have your face all frosted up with the snow. By Jiminy, it's a cold one up there in

the winter time. (*How long does the cold last?*) Oh, they have two seasons up

there, they tell us, you know, from the summer into winter, there, but the real cold

starts around Thanksgiving time and lasts all the way into June.

(*Ah, what happens around in March?*) Well, then—we start to get what they call

up there, "Mud Vacation," when the spring breakup comes, and all the frost comes

out of the roads and it thaws a little bit, and it runs off and the Mississippi floods,

(*ah*) and so then the little town of Aiken, there, has been under water many, many times, especially on the north side. (*How many times?*) Many, many times, especially on the north side of the town. (*Ah, yes. Why the north side?*) Well, that's where the river runs. . . .

(*Were you born on the farm or in the town?*) Well, I was born in a rural area, and then we—when I was in the—ah, around the fifth grade, we moved into the town itself, but we were, ah—we had a cow and about 26 chickens, ah, there. (*Was it your job to milk the cow?*) No, I never could do that. I couldn't get any milk out, no matter how hard I squeezed. I fed the chickens now and gathered the eggs and split the wood, and that kind of stuff, ya. [*What kind of stock did you have?*] [We had] Guernsey cows and we had Rhode Island Red chickens. No—no, I think there might have been one Leghorn around there, but he was the rooster. Ya, ya, son of a gun, he jumped around all the time, and enjoyed himself a lot in the chicken yard. . . .

One thing I wanted to tell you about was there, ah, there was this Swedish couple up there, they had a baby, and they were trying to decide what it was they should name this little girl, and the daddy, he wanted to name her Violet, but he couldn't say Violet, so they called her Genevieve instead.

NORWAY

Title #2: The donor of the next transcript, a hunting and fishing guide in western Canada, was taped beside his cabin, off the regular road by many miles. His accent is a very modest one compared with the Swedish transcript. The [ɛʳ] (*air*) vowel gets a vigorous treatment, and a *w* for *v* can be heard in *development* and *volcano.* In addition, the rural American tendency to drop the *g* from *ing,* once so prevalent and now heard less and less often, is quite obvious at the beginning of the transcript. The Scandinavian lilt or melodic inflection is suggested rather than accomplished.

The Wilderness Guide

. . . (*And how long have you been in this country?*) I came here in 1937. (*And what, what is your occupation?*) Guide—hunting, fishing, trapping, a little farming now and then. (*Now, when you go out on a trip what do you do?*) Well, in summer time we go on fishing trips, you know, into the big lakes and rivers—the trout, trout fishing mostly. Winter time, fall rather, we go after the moose, caribou, deer, elk. (*Caribou?*) Oh, ya. (*Are there caribou up in this country?*) Oh, ya, we got caribou up here now. They disappeared in, ah, the winter of '37. And now they are coming back again, so we have quite a few around now. . . . (*Were you born in this country?*) No, no, I was born in Norway. Ya, I came here in 1930.

(*Doesn't it get pretty cold up here?*) No, we had only one cold winter since I came in here, and that was, ah, I think it was '48. (*How cold does it get?*) Well, then it dropped to 60 below. (*60 below!*) Ya, that's cold. It warmed up to 40 there in the middle of the day, you know, but it stayed around 60 for a week.

. . . (*What do you think about the country and its possibilities for development?*) Oh, it's going to be a lot of development in here years to come, ya, I think. (*Any minerals in here?*) Not here, not here in the Myrtle River country. It's all covered with volcanic ash, you know, the whole works. (*Oh, I see. Volcanic ash?*) Ya, several volcanoes up in here of recent origin.

DENMARK

Title #3: The following transcript provides a good illustration of an accent that has only a few key sounds in it, all of which are easily detected. It is a strong accent nonetheless. Unlike its companions, Swedish and Norwegian speech, it has no melodic inflection at all. It does, however, have a strong uvular *r*. Also, while a *v* is substituted occasionally for *w* or *wh,* the process is often reversed with a *w* for a *v,* as in *government* and *Viking.*

This transcript was taped in a cabin in northern British Columbia.

A Dane in B.C.

I was born in Denmark, in a place called Albor, and that's on a peninsula called Jutland. And I spent all my—my boyhood there, and I went to school and went to university, and later on joined the army, which we all have to do for 18 months. And after that I went to Greenland, which is part of Denmark. (*Oh, what did you do in Greenland?*) I was, ah, working for the government—in Denmark the government had a monopoly on the trade.

(*Incidentally, Nik, where did the name Greenland come from? There's nothing green there, is there?*) No, not at all, except on the southern part. But maybe it's a sales gimmick, you know, a way of selling real estate, and when Erik the Red, or whatever his name was, came back from this trip and—(*Who was that?*) I think it was Erik the Red, who was a Viking. When he came back from this trip, ah, he had to tell about the country, and he wanted other people to come with him on the next trip so he could settle. Now, if he called it, you know, said it was all snow and ice, nobody would go with him. But if he called it Greenland, well maybe somebody could.

(*Well, then, after, after Greenland, what?*) Well, we came back to Denmark for about a year, and then we left for Canada.

(*You were, for a long period of time, you were the official guide for this area, were you not? How was the guiding done? What did that entail?*) Well, it entails, you—you make an agreement with somebody to take them on a hunt at a certain time, hunting certain animals. And it's, ah, very demanding, a quite difficult job at times. What bothers me the most is the way people handle their firearms. They will

load the magazine up, they will put a round in the chamber, and then they will

walk with their guns in their hands, you know, as if you were walking in Vietnam

and expecting an enemy to—to jump you. And this is, of course, not very good.

They say in the books that the guide goes ahead, you know, the white guide, and

look over the country and, and the clients follow. But as far as I'm concerned, I

walk behind.

THE NETHERLANDS

Title #4: The immigrant of the next selection, a long-time resident of
western Canada, was very glad to talk about his language background. In
addition to the stock key sounds he has been using for years, you may
note his pronunciation of the word *southern:* His diphthong is exactly the
same as that of the Dane in Title #3, who employed it for the same word.

There are three simple key sounds to note: the hard *r* [ř], which can be
altered as described, the *v* for *w,* and the *d* for *th.* Also, an *s* for *z* (*because*)
might be employed.

The Dutch ''R''

(*You were telling me about the play of the* r *in speech in various parts of the*

Netherlands. Would you develop that a little bit more?) Well, I'll try [v] any[ř][v]way,

be[s]cause if you listen to a man that o[ř]riginally comes from Amsterdam or Rotter[ř]dam,

you'll find [d]that there i[s]s a faint [ř]roll of the [d]r, if he speaks Dutch, and sometimes this

is carried on if he starts speaking English, and in some people it is more distinct

than in other people. But the [d]rolling of the r, the [v]way [→]they do it from those two

particular places in Holland, is usually done with the tip of the tongue. Now in the

southern part of Holland, when we get closer to the Belgian border, the roll is there far more distinct, but it comes more out of the throat area than out of the tip of the tongue.

Now in the northern part of Holland, in the Friesian area, and actually the Friesian area and the people there speak a definite different language that is totally different, and not related at all to the rest of the Dutch language.

(*Which city were you born in?*) I was born in Rotterdam. (*And you grew up there?*) And I grew up in Rotterdam and, ah, I was 21 when I left, so I've been trying to speak English for the last 26 years, the hard way.

Title #5: In addition to the key sounds that will be heard in the next transcript, an unusual handling of the *r* will also be apparent. At times it will be trilled with the front of the tongue, but in other instances it will be given a very muscular treatment, causing it to sound quite hard. Vocabulary and word order also will attract your attention.

A Lonely Immigrant

[A question was asked about the first days in a new country.] You felt—you really lonely, you know, and I found English then so cold, you know, so cold. It didn't say me any, there was no—you see, I was always scared that I would say the wrong thing (*yes*) and especial the Canadian expression in his English is different what we learned at school from London. I was flabbergast and I was amazed at, I never learned this. . . . (*Now you think in English, do you not?*) Right. I'm not thinking more in—in, from the old country. But before, I often—you were, now, talking to me, I would translate it. (*Yes.*) I don't do it more, because I can just, just fluently follow what you mean.

(*You were talking about the English language in contrast to the Netherlands.*) Ya, the contrast is there. But the English speak the sound right in front of the mouth. The tongue does a lot to vocalize, to form the word, but it is right in front

of the mouth. But the sound of the language of the Netherlands, and the Friesian

language, and the German language, that is formed in the throat. So that it is

different. So that for the immigrants from my country, we have to learn to bring the

words more in front of the mouth. We have to use the tongue more. (*The tip of the*

tongue.) The tip of the tongue to get loose, so that we can form the words better.

But that is harder for us. We, we have to, ah, again like to go back to our mother

[language] and learn on—on the foot the language, to speak it proper.

AUSTRIA

Title #6: Once, in a group of Austrians, the statement was made that in reality, Austrian speech was just another German regional dialect; the remark did not elicit an agreeable response, but rather just the opposite and in strength. Be that as it may, from the point of view of a dialect student, the key sounds, allowing for individual differences, are essentially the same for an Austrian as for a German accent. The remarks of the first voice that you will hear, for example, supplies us with a checklist that matches in detail the one given at the beginning of this series. The donor, a visitor from Austria, was taped in a cabin in a small town in western Canada; the sounds of an impending fish fry are heard in the background.

The VW

. . . I work in the city of Salzburg, yes. I was born in Vienna and I go to school in

Vienna till 19 years, the age from 19 years, and then I began work. I—(*What kind of*

work did you do?) Ah, in the bureau [office], and I was in Germany for about half, a

half-year in a firm, and now I work at 10 years, about 10 years for a, for a firm

handling with cars. (*What kind of cars?*) Volkswagen and Audi. You

know—(*yes*)—the Audi?

[A question was asked about VW exports to the States.] Two years ago they have many problems, ah, with the exports to the States, you know, ah, the price was very high, and the Japanese cars was, were cheaper in, ah, in America and in the States, and now they built a factory in U.S.A., and they want to build the Rabbit in the States, and then the car will be cheaper, and the, it, now they have no problems in Germany. [*I understand they are going to do away with the famous little car.*] No-no-no-no, you mean the Beetle? (*Yes, the Beetle.*) Oh, the Beetle, ah, is built now in Mexico and in Brazilia, and not in, ah, Europe because there is no necessary for it.

Title #7: The following transcript, which is handicapped because it is read rather than spoken in dialogue form, was taped many years ago in the kitchen of a hotel in the Austrian Alps; work sounds are heard in the background. The reading itself caused some interesting responses. The donor, a cook with limited schooling in English, remembered to pronounce each *w* as *w,* just as he was taught to do when he read in class. However, as I was speaking with him during the moments before the taping, he pronounced *w* or *wh* with the *v* we have come to expect. Also, before and after the reading, he said *da* instead of *the,* and each *and* was either *ant* or *unt.*

The Red Auto

We were just walking down the road, my friends and I, when I first saw the great big motorcar coming towards us very fast. It was painted a shiny red color, like the material the girls put on their fingernails. What made the episode so startling was that neither I nor my friends could see anybody at the wheel. It just seemed to come around the corner without any driver at all, and head straight for us. I think someone, perhaps Rosina, or maybe one of the other girls made a big scream. Whoever it was must have been standing very close to me, for the sound came right in my ear. Then someone else, and it might have been me, let out a large shout. If I were the one who shouted, I know I must have been trying to tell the big

motorcar to get back on the right side of the road. Then, suddenly, just before it

came to us, it swerved across the center line and went on to its own side of the

road.[3]

GERMANY

Title #8, East Germany: One aspect of the Teutonic accent that is not treated in *Stage Dialects* and not included so far in this book, is the substitution of *z* for *s,* as it is heard in a limited number of regional dialects. To illustrate this usable sound—it has good comedic possibilities—the following short excerpt is offered. The donor, a German, is a native of Silesia, a province located in what used to be the eastern section of old Germany. This same substitution, interestingly enough, was made by the Dutch donor of "A Lonely Immigrant" when he spoke of the title of an old Dutch poem, which he called "Zinging and Playing" (Singing and Playing).

The Teutonic "Z" for "S"

. . . We came from Germany to the United States several months ago. Now we are

going to read for you in English as an illustration of a German accent. First we will

give some single words. We will say the word first, then pause a little while so that

you may repeat the word, then we will say it again. . . .

[The donor reads.] I came here for an explanation, but since you refuse to tell

me yourself, I will tell you. I thought I could trust you, Ida. I thought you were really

grateful for all I have tried to do for you. But I see I have been made a fool of, and I

object to it. . . .

[3] This script, used also in *Stage Dialects,* was designed to give full play to the key sounds of a Teutonic accent.

SPAIN

Title #9: Many Americans, especially those of us who live in the southwest, think of the Spanish language and the Spanish accent as it comes to us across the Mexican border. As a result, when Americans are in Spain itself, they listen in vain for the cadences and inflections that they have associated with Spanish speech and accent.

There are similarities of pronunciation, of course, between the Spanish spoken in Spain and in Mexico.

There are many of these similarities—the [ɛ] (*eh*) added in front of an initial [s], as when a Spaniard calls his or her own country *España* instead of Spain, or the half [b]/half [v] sound that is scored phonetically as [β]—but a comparison between this first Spanish title, "The Man Behind the Desk," and the first Chicano title, "The Mechanic," will disclose the differences as well.

The accent of the donor is the result of both study in school and exposure and practice abroad (a commonplace circumstance for many Europeans, especially those engaged in hotel work), since the speaker has worked his way through a good portion of the English-speaking world. While the accent is obvious, it also is limited in strength and fluency. The key sounds are easily noted.

The Man Behind the Desk

. . . I live in ' Irun, and, ah, this hotel is in Frontravia, near France, near the border, about 14 kilometers from France and, ah, is a very beauti' ful place in, up in the moun' tain, is about four hundred ninety meters—the river, the sea is about a half-kilometer from here, and the bea' ches are very beauti' ful beaches all around, and the fishing town, and the ' Irun is a frontier so—(*Fishing? The hotel guests can go fishing?*) Yeah, they can go fishing to the ri' ver or to the sea, anywhere on the rocks, behind us in the moun' tains. (*Oh, yes.*) Yeah, you can see Biarritz from here, nice place, place to, you know, to—(*lose your money*—) to lose your money.

Title #10: The donor of the next selection was coaxed out of his kitchen long enough to offer an accent whose basis is founded in hotel talk: rooms, sittings, and foods. Not heard in the preceding title and just barely apparent in this one is the very common and usable sound of *d* before *y*, as when *yes* is pronounced *dyes* [dzjɛs]. There will be no lack of this sound elsewhere, however, as it will be heard strongly and clearly in the Chicano and the Puerto Rican transcripts.

The Chef

[When was this parador built?] This is finish on the twenty-six last May. (*And how many rooms does it have?*) Ah, is 31 lovely beds. [*And is it popular?*] Yes, on the summer is come about 60 or 70 percent, is the strangers peoples. (*Should*—) And now, and now in the winter, the same.

[*You have worked outside of Spain?*] Yes, I work the chef on Wales, for five summers on the Rockpile Hotel on Llandrindod, Wales. . . . Seventy rooms—(*70 rooms*), ah, about 140 sittings on the dining room. (*And every summer you went back, just for the summer?*) Yes, I work on the summer. I back to see the family in the spring. (*Ah, yes, you have a family here?*) Yes, I have the one daughter, 5 years old, and another one, another three-quarters now (*ah, yes*), another one is come.

PORTUGAL

Title #11: Portugal, a small country on the extreme southwest tip of Europe, has a language that is distinctively its own. This fact, however, does not produce for us a unique kind of accent; instead, the quite usual syllabic substitutions will be heard on the tape—a *d* for *th*, a dropped *h*, and the alteration of a few vowels.

More distinctive is the elimination of the [j] sound, as heard in the word *usually*, and a change of emphasis or stress from a first to a second or third syllable, as in *situ'ated* and *comfor'table*. Then, at the very end of the tape, the *ed* of the past tense of a verb is pronounced (as it often is elsewhere in Europe).

The donor is a clerk in one of the new and very comfortable state-owned posadas that cater to the tourist trade.

A Kind of Inn

. . . Well, this is kind of a inn, ah, belongs to state, and it's usually situa'ted in

very well lo'cated places, outside of towns and village where is very quiet and, ah,

almost with all of them are comfor'table. (*This then, was planned not to be in a*

town or, or a city, but along the road?) Right, along the road, and a place where

there is a view, a nice view and things like it. (*Now how old is this—*) This has

been up in for almost 18 months. It has 10, I mean, 17 rooms. (*17—*) Yes, all of

them with twin beds, bathroom, telephone, ea'ting, and all comfor'table things that

usually in this kind of place, has to be. . . .

(*Now this is a—this is, ah, run by the state?*) Right, yes. I mean it's run—this

belongs to state, but it's run by private, a, by a private—(*company?*) right. Not

company, it can be company, but usually by a private professional hostelry.

(*Where did you learn to speak English?*) Ah, in school, in Portugal. Of course I

went to England and I went—I have been in States as well, so I practice a bit

around. (*So you worked in England, did you?*) Oh, well, I worked for a few months,

yes, and I worked in States also. Then from there I went to Central America, to

Mexico and all those countries around—tripping!

Title #12: The following short transcript comes from the receptionist in
the Posada Estramoz, one of the most interesting and beautiful places to
stay in all of Europe. For all its shortness, the piece contains several
interesting key sounds, for example, an *r* trilled with the back of the
tongue and the pronunciations of *Queen* and *King*. The rapid speech is a
personal characteristic, and obviously some of the material has been
memorized.

Estramoz

. . . Well, I am receptionist at the Posada Reina Santa Isabella, and I work here

every days. (*And where is the posada located? What is the name of the country here that*—?) Estramoz, the name of the country, Estramoz, yes, and the name of the posada, Reina Santa Isabella. (*And what—would you describe the posada?*) Well, before the [previously] the posada is a castle, with the Reina Santa Isabella and King Dominic. Reina Santa Isabella is a Spanish queen, yes, and King Dominic is a Portuguese [*king*] queen. Ah, they married here in the premiere, queen of English (?) but here at Estramoz, in the thirteenth century Renaissance.

Posada Reina Santa Isabella is a—was a—is a posada, is very nice posada. I think the most nice in Europe. (*I agree.*) The nicest of Portugal—(*Yes, and Europe as well*) Yes.

ITALY

Title #13: As stated in my introductory remarks to this chapter, there is no intent to offer any of those major accents that have been presented already in *Stage Dialects.* However, this short sequence from the Italian is included here with special justification; its subject matter is as much of sociological as dialectal interest. As you will hear, it reveals a wholly new explanation as to why so many emigrants left their countries to come to the United States.

A Better Box

. . . When I retire I would like to spend a couple of years in Italy, in my own land, because, you know, if you scraped my heart you find a piece of Italy in there. (*Where will you go in Italy? To your hometown?*) No, my hometown, no, because my hometown is still left the way it was, behind the age. I like move near Rome, which I got relatives over there. I like have a house, which is already a built house, right there. Then spend a couple of years. But nevertheless, I think I like a die in the United States, because it is a rich land, and I think I get a better, better box.

Greece and Eastern Europe

Including Yugoslavia, Hungary, Romania, Czechoslovakia, Poland, Lithuania

Greece, geographically located south of and immediately adjacent to Yugoslavia, is included in this grouping of Eastern European countries simply for reasons of spacing on the tape. Certainly there is no political alignment or identification with the Warsaw Pact nations; Greece's affiliations in this respect are entirely with Western Europe and the United States.

Nor is there any connection with the Slavic language base that is common to all of the countries directly to the north, with the exception of Romania. Greece has her own distinct lingual identity, which is respected and honored, revered even, throughout the Western World.

This is not to say that there are no similarities between the key sounds of a Greek accent and those of other nations. As we have seen repeatedly, the number of distinct vowel, diphthong, and consonant formations that make up any dialect or accent is limited, and often they are very similar. This is true in the case of Greece.

Here are the key sound substitutions that pertain to all the speakers in this section, the Greek and Eastern European donors alike.

1. The [i] of *eat* replaces the [ɪ] of *it*, making *it* sound like *eat*, and *this is it* becomes *thees ees eat*.

2. The voiced *th* [ð] as in *that* or *these* is replaced by [d], the result of which is *dat* and *dese*.

3. The [ɛʳ] of *air* replaces the [ɜ˞] of *her*, so that *her* sounds like *hair*; and usually the [r] will have a single tongue tap or a slight trill with the front of the tongue.

4. The [r] is often single tapped or trilled with the front of the tongue; sometimes it is done so easily that it is difficult to detect.

5. The consonant [ḣ] is sometimes heavily aspirated, giving it a very breathy sound. Since there is no [h] in the Slavic language, the Slavs, who are

not accustomed to forming it, make an extra effort to make the sound by a rush of air against the hump of the back of the tongue. You will hear this in the Yugoslav transcript. It is also present in a Greek accent although, by chance, it is not as heavily performed as could be wished.

6. The present participle *ing* can be given a hard [g] or [k] ending, making *running* ['rʌnɪŋg], *runninga* ['rʌnɪŋg], or *runningk* ['rʌnɪŋk].

7. Very often the *ed* of a verb in the past tense will be pronounced as the terminal syllable. Thus, *walked* ['wɔkt] becomes ['wɔkɛd].

GREECE

Out of an extensive amount of material taped on several occasions, two short sections have been selected for this transcript, each of which offers interesting content as well as a distinctively illustrated accent.

In addition to the key sounds listed above, two additional ones are to be noted in "Socrates" and "War"; that is, *guard* is pronounced *gyuard* ['qiʌrd], which is quite a Russian sound, and *bomb* has the plosive [b] sounded twice, as in ['bamb] instead of ['bam]. This demonstrates a tendency, not unusual with those who speak English with a foreign accent, to pronounce syllables that have long been dropped in ordinary usage.

However, it is not only the key sounds that you will hear on the tape, as distinct and attractive as they are, which gives this particular accent its distinction and makes it one of the finest in the book. The donor, a Greek actor (and now a life-long friend), is self-taught in English. From this informal training come the elements of word choice and word order that result in a distinguished delivery, which is both expressive and informative. Add to these the action of very flexible articulators and you have a precision of speech that in itself gives distinction to the accent.

Title #1: The following two short transcripts were taped in my own home as we attempted to repay the many kindnesses our friend had shown us each time we were in Athens. The talk centered on the recent discoveries that relocated the famous prison where Socrates spent his last hours.

Socrates' Prison

[Socrates' prison is a building which] is square and long, and one side is narrower

than the other. It consists from one court where the prisoners they used to go out to

walk, and four rooms one side, I think, and three rooms the other side, the prison.

And one of the rooms, was in the middle, has a little terra-cotta basin, small

terra-cotta basin, like a huge vase, you know. There they used to go to wash. And

the floors, they have changed many times. The beginning was soil, clay. And then,

during probably the Romans, they used to do that mosaic, different periods. And in

the entrance of the building on the left, ah, ah, hand as you get in, there is two store building where used to be the guard, was higher than the other building, you

know. . . .

(*But how did they know it was the prison of Socrates?*) Oh, they know because

of the descriptions and details which they compare, which they put down

altogether from one writer to the other writer, they put it down, what one says, what

the other says, what descriptions are, what religion is, and then they make

conclusions, you know, according to the holes, according to the style of the

building, anyway finally they said this is the prison of Socrates—

War

(*You were in Athens during the war, during the German occupation?*) Yes, I was in

Athens the time the war started, and I remember the day the first airplane came, I

mean enemy's airplane, Italian airplanes was flying high up over the Greece,

probably to observe what is going down there, you know, and everyone was still, I

mean cool, but slowly and gradually, you know, they started to—the *sirenas,* the

sirens, you say, to whistling, and in danger everyone starts to run on the streets to

go under the big buildings to protect themselves. That was the war, and the

bombing. I remember the bombing on Piraeus, the last days the airplanes, the

German airplanes, like wasps they used to come—a million, million, one of waves

after one, one after one, the waves, many airplanes to go to bomb the Piraeus, the

last days, . . . and I have from Piraeus bombing one night was hell, I mean the

whole Athens was bright from the fires and the bombing, you know, and the noise

and the rain—. . . .

Eastern Europe is the home of the Slavic languages, and the discussion here deals almost entirely with those buffer nations that Russia has established between herself and the European states. With the exception of Yugoslavia, they are the Warsaw Pact countries, and although the native language of each differs from that of the others, when any individual from any one of them speaks in English, all employ a good number of the same key sounds. This is true even of the Romanian voice that you will hear, although Romania herself derives her language from the Latin rather than the Slavic (the Roman legionnaires settled on that fertile land in large numbers).[1]

In addition to the key sounds previously listed

[1] For a fuller exposition of this subject, see Chapter XIII, "Russia," in Jerry Blunt, *Stage Dialects* (New York: Harper & Row, 1967).

for this area, there are three to be added:

1. The substitution of [v] for [w] or *wh* [hw], that is, *vas* for *was* or *vich* for *which*, undoubtedly is the most common and most recognizable of any of the key sound changes. Unless the speaker has been trained by much practice—many of them have—he or she will make this substitution over and over again.

2. The voiceless *th* [θ], as in *think*, is replaced by a single [t], so that *think* becomes *tink*.

3. The [ɑu] diphthong, as in *ouch* [ɑutʃ], may be substituted for the vowel [ɔ], as in *pause* [pɔz], so that *pause* becomes *pouwz* [pɑuz].

YUGOSLAVIA

Title #2: The following donor, a typewriter repairman from Yugoslavia who has been in the United States since 1957, was taped on my college campus. It is not often that the owner of a fine dialect walks into your office and is willing to talk into a microphone. Needless to say, the typewriter that required attention waited in silence.

The most unusual and usable element in the following transcript is the unique word order that the donor relies on for the expression of his thoughts. It is especially noteworthy because his delivery has a relatively free flow and a sustained continuity. The confusion of verb tenses also adds distinction, as does the use or the nonuse of articles.

In contrast, the key sounds of the accent are not as numerous or as strongly uttered as is usual in speech that sounds as good as this one does. Obviously, the donor has worked harder on his pronunciation than on his grammar. At any rate, he has given us a fine transcript.

Here are the key sound substitutions to listen for: the heavily separated [ħ], the [i] for [ɪ], a [g] or [k] ending for *ing*, a slight tapped [rʳ], the [v] for [w] or *wh* [hw].

"Seven Day" Adventist

I am born in Yugoslavia. (*Ah, and did you spend most of your childhood there?*)

　　　　　　　　　　　　　　　i i
Yes, I spent till 32 years. . . . I left from religion problem. I am Seven Day

　　　　i i　　　ħ　　　　　　　　　　　　ħ
Adventist religion. And I had too much troubles over there, because he don't let

　　　　　　　　　　　　　　　　　　ɔ　　　　　　　　ɔ
you to believe what you want. He say he is the God, and I know just one God, and

ħ   i   ɔ   ħ i ħ   ħ

he—who is the living God for everybody. Who is on heaven. Some people who

i   i   i

today live, for today's own position and tomorrow is nothing they want.

(*Now, you say, he. Did you mean the ruler, ah*—) The rulers, yeah. (*Who are the*

I

rulers?) Tito was. (*Tito. And a very strong government control, was there?*) Oh, yes.

               gə   rʳ   ħ   rʳ gə

He's still a very strong government control. Just right now, how I am hearing, is

i   i i   ħ   →

little softly for, softly [easier] for the religion. Not like before, when he was with

Russia.

(*Were you—was it easy for you to get out, away from the country?*) No, was not

easy, no. Was some exhibition open, for people who has master's degree, in

Munich, West Germany. And I got to this visa and I went out and I don't come back

anymore. . . . Oh, I went right away in United Nations camp, and I apply—apply

for the immigration, and I got it to come in United States. After year and a half I got

my wife and children—(*Oh, they let them come out to join you?*) Yeah, because,

ah, over there is many women and not men, you know. He [Tito], he looking for

manpower. He don't care too much for women powers. . . .

(*How do you like your life now?*) Oh, I like very much. I am enjoying—(*good*)—

nobody bother me for religion. (*Ah, yes.*) I am free and in a free country, I believe in,

and I feel I am.

HUNGARY

Title #3: The next transcript was taped in a speech clinic where the donor
was taking a class in English pronunciation. The slow pace, the result of
her commendable effort to form all the sounds properly, gives the listener
the best chance yet to analyze and transcribe the key sounds of her
accent. Obviously, she has made progress: her speech is not as desirably
strong in the beginning as it is later on in the tape.
    The key sounds to be noted are: [i] for [ɪ], [v] for [w] or [hw] (she
wanted to give a [w] for [v] on *very*, which is another fairly common

substitution), and [ɛʳ] for [ɜʳ], [d] for the voiced *th* [ð], [k] on *ing* [ŋk], and [rʳ] slightly tapped.

Lady *from* Budapest

I came from Hungary. (*Where in Hungary?*) I living in Bubapest. My parents also live in Budapest. I live here about 3 years. I am married. My husband is also Hungary—Hungary—Hungarian man. He speak English very well. He live here about 20 years ago. I am housewife. I don't work here. I worked—my country—I worked on the ' computer, I work IBM computer and French computer. But I didn't work here.

(*Would you tell me about Budapest?*) Budapest is beautiful city, and the river is also beautiful, and Buda—Buda, and Pest, two town. Buda is old town, city, city, Buda—Pest is modern. (*Can you tell me something about its history? Who was your national hero?*) Hero? In—we have not hero. We have king, and we big king in, was, ah, Stephen, king. He was very good man—. . .

I am very nervous! I am forget everything. You know, is terrible feeling, this—is terrible—"it," I can't, ah, making, you know. "It," "it" is very hard for me—(*Now what about—*)—the short sounds—"it" and "cookbook!" (*What about the "r?"*) "Rrrh" is English, and in Hungary, Hungarian language "r" [is] "er." But in Hungarian language we have not "th" voiceless, and "th" voiced, and we have not a, a short sound, and my trouble also "w," "w—," "would" and "women"—to move my mouth is terrible. [My] trouble is, ah, I can't speak English because I am alone my house, because my husband work all day. I—I have not enough practice in speech, and I try listen to TV and radio, but is not enough for me.

Title #4: The following selection was taped as we sat—the young woman, her friends, and I—in the huge, empty and very quiet Budapest football (soccer) stadium.

The speaker of the previous tape is a native of Hungary who is now living in the United States and just beginning her language study. This donor, a native of Budapest, had just completed an advanced English language course with high marks. The result is that this tape, in contrast to the previous one, presents a moderate accent with good word choice and word order, delivered at a pace that suggests memorization of the subject material. Yet she was not an official guide but only a friend who liked to show visitors around.

Although the donor has worked on her pronunciation (note her control of her "r's"), there are still key sounds to be transcribed: the voiceless and voiced *th* [θ] and [ð], respectively, which become [t] in *thousand* [' tauznd] and [d] in *the* [da]; the [i] for [ɪ] in *lived* [' lɪvd], making [' lɪvd]; the [g] or [k] added to *ing* [ŋ] in *king* [' kɪŋ], making [' kɪŋk]; the usual [v] for [w]; and once a [w] for [v].

Lady *in* Budapest

[In the first of the fourth century] the Roman legions settled down and they lived up here—up there until the end of the fourth century. From the fourth up to the ninth century different tribes are marching through the country. The Avars, the Huns, the Goths, and we, the Hungarians, came here at the end of the ninth century only, with the leadership of Arpad—he was a chieftain of the Hungarian clan of the Hungarian tribe.

And we crowned our first king, Saint Stephen in 1000 and he introduced Christianity, and founded the Hungarian state. And from Arpad being the chieftain of the Hungarian clan, every Hungarian king came from the Arpad house, and our last king from the Arpad house died in thirteen and seven. His name was, ah, Andrea, it's a Hungarian name. And then in 1241 we had a Tartar invasion, and King Bela IV was on the throne at the time, and he built the royal palace to defend the Hungarians against the new Tartar invasion.

And I think our most, and most popular and most famous king was Matthew. He was set to be a king on the ice of the Danube, and he was elected by the peasants. And during his reign, Hungary was the most richest in her long history.

ROMANIA

Title #5· The donor in the next selection, well educated and proficient in several languages, is presently the owner of a factory in West Germany. He was taped in a cabin in northern British Columbia—the dinner dishes are being washed nearby—at the end of a day of trophy hunting.

   The usual key sounds are to be noted, even though the accent is actually less strong than it seems. Attention should be paid to the vowel [ε^r], as heard later in *border*. This particular pronunciation is much more common in Eastern Europe than the tapes have so far demonstrated.

The Maize Field

   . . . I am refugee coming from formerly Austrian-Hungarian monarchy $\overset{v}{w}h\overset{i}{i}ch$

became—$\overset{v}{w}h\overset{i}{i}ch$ part o$\overset{f}{f}$ the, of Hungaria became later Romania. . . . [*You were in*

Romania until when?] Until August, 1944, $\overset{v}{w}hen$ the Russian army came to

$\overset{r^r}{R}$omania. (*And then you went*—?) I went for Hungary first, and then, seeing that

even Hungary $\overset{vi}{w}ill$ be occupied in a short time, ah, $\overset{v}{w}e$ passed the

Hungarian-Austrian border. . . .

   (*You were able, did you have any difficulty getting transportation in those*

days?) Humm—more than difficulties. It was quite terrible. Ah, when I decided, or I

decided with my wife, to go away, first $\overset{v}{w}e$ had to d$\overset{\varepsilon^r}{r}\overset{v}{i}ve$—not to d$\overset{r^r}{r}ive$. We had no

car for th$\overset{i}{i}s$ time. We had to ride the train from the middle of Romania to the fron$\overset{t\int r}{t}ier$.

My—my native country $\overset{i}{i}s$ near to the $\overset{d}{}$fron$\overset{t\int r}{t}$i$\vec{e}r$, my native town. (*Yes.*) Then we

couldn't get other cars than open cars for cattle. So the trouble began

immediately. And then how to pass—how to pass the border.

   The second difficulty was how to pass the border because it could happen that

we try to pass the border—the border, for example, how we did it in a maize—we

went, ah, through a maize—how do you call this high corn (*yes*), maize? (*Maize.*)

Maize, a culture of maize higher than we were, and we had to pass something like

2 miles, because moving, this maize, it would be possible that—that we will—that

we will—that we will be killed. We couldn't see anything. We passed on an

evening and when we were in Yugoslavia, we heard that even there it's not allowed

to travel after six o'clock.

. . . [Finally, in answer to a question about the *r* of that area—] Because look

at one thing—I can speak *r-r-r,* I can speak *r,* but I am speaking with *er-r* [ɛʳ],

because this is typical, typical for all people in Eastern Europe, I think.

CZECHOSLOVAKIA

Title #6: The donor of the following selection was a Czech official in the Dubchek government who left his country as a result of that party's policy of harassment. He is speaking at a panel discussion in London.

There is a mixture in his accent that varies somewhat from the previous Eastern European donors. He sounds as if there might be a German influence (not unusual) in the [t] for [d] in the first *and* and an [s] for [z] in *because.* There is also a French influence, for example, the [z] for the voiced *th* [ð] in *the* and a change of stress in *pro'ducts.* However, he also uses a [d] for the voice *th* in *the* [dʌ], and this is commonplace. The other key sounds are the usual ones: a [k] on *ing,* a [v] for [w], the [ɛʳ] (*air*) for [ɜʳ] (*her*) in *workers,* and a slightly tapped [rʳ]. There is an unusual pronunciation of the word *plan,* but this seems to be an individual characteristic.

Economic Refugee

. . . it's enough to take the companies and the prizes off of the capitalists, to

introduce, ah, central planning of the whole economy, on the whole that would be

all right. But, ah, very soon the experience came back to—because you have in

the industrial deve'lopment country hundred and hundred thousand, I would say

mil,lions, in Czechoslovakia we got counted with one and a half mil,lions of

con'crete pro'ducts, kinds of pro'ducts. And this means, if a—if a central planning committee should really plan all this concrete kind of product, this would mean the

plan, that this—cannot be prepared, even with the most modern computer system

you cannot plan it, because this are so—so much interrelationships that you would

prepare such a plan. . . .

[A question was asked about the human element, the relationship between

workers and management.] Oh, I would say that the relation between the workers

and the management is a relation between, I would say, bureaucratics and

working people. That the enterprises are more alienated to the workers than in the

West. The—the workers have not the right, no, no interest of the managing of the

enterprises, because this are—this are strange plans, this are strange aims, they

are only interested in their wages.

Title #7: The following donor was taped in a speech clinic where she had
come for help, not only with the new language of English, but also for
guidance on a speech problem: a hesitancy aggravated by a blockage. In
this instance her difficulty was made more acute by the subject matter: a
vivid recall of a very exciting experience. She has already accomplished
several noteworthy corrections of her accent, as you will notice, so that it
has to be classed as moderate rather than strong.

Airplanes in the Night

I came from Czechoslovakia. I was born in Presborg, is on the border of a—a

Austria. (*Why did you come here to this country?*) Well, I, you know, there was a

kind of revolution, the Russians said that there was supposed to be kind of

revolution, and so they—they came there to prevented the revolution. But, but we

were at this time very peaceful people and we didn't want—we didn't know about

any revolution. But one night a—about 12 o'clock midnight we saw—we heard many

airplanes on top of our—our houses. And it, it—they weren't ordinary airplanes, they were airplanes which—[had come from Moscow.] (*Did they drop bombs?*) No, they didn't drop bombs. But in the morning we wake up and it was very unpleasant to see—to see around our house full of soldiers, and they were every man [everywhere] confusement, very confused. They—they did not know where they are, which place they are, and a, they saw a very confused people in—the soldiers were outside looking and—we didn't have the few times the bread in the stores because the soldiers ate the bread. So it was kind of, you know, funny experience.

POLAND

Title #8: National borders to the contrary, dialectal differences do not vary significantly among nationalities that have the same language base. Rather, the relative strength or weakness of the accent, as evidenced by the number of detectable key sounds, the vocabulary size (a limited choice of words in the new language, allowing only confused or vague expressions, in contrast to a wider range that permits more precise meanings), and a word order or a sentence structure that is in disarray or, in reverse, is neatly aligned, determine the noticeable prescence and distinguishing characteristics of an accent.

The basis for this belief will be demonstrated by the contrast exhibited between the next two titles. Although both donors are Polish—and related by marriage—the first will be heard speaking with a moderate accent, in which all elements, that is, key sounds, word choice, and word order, are in markedly better shape than those in the second title.

Although the donor of the following selection has been in her new country, Canada, only a couple of years, she previously had studied English as a part of her formal schooling in her native land. She was taped in her own home in a very small town in northern British Columbia, making, I think, provocative statements that merit consideration.

Afterwards she led me across the road to meet an older man who had been in Canada since 1964 but who had given no time, thought, or practice to the acquisition of any skill in the language of his new country. Because he lived in a family enclave where Polish was spoken almost exclusively, his skill was manual (he operated a huge debarking machine in the local lumber mill) and not lingual.

Few key sounds will be heard in the sections of dialogue of Title #8, although the usual ones—[i] for [ɪ], [v] for [w], [d] for *th,* and [k] added to *ing*—were in evidence in those portions not included here. The usual beginning phonetic transcriptions will not appear.

A Contrast in Values

[*What part of your native country are you from?*] The southeast part of Poland. I—I was born in little village, Brzeziny. (*Brajena—how would you spell it?*) Oh, gee, it's *Brzeziny.*[2]

. . . [She was asked about the ease of life in present-day Poland.] It isn't an easy life, but I think Polish people are more happy in their, in, well, inside more happy than people in here. This—I don't know. I—I—I found it here that people in here trouble, are very troubled, how to get money, how to arrange to have the house and car, and they are, they think a lot about material problems and kinds, and can't enjoy themselves inside.

I don't know, maybe I'm not right, but it came to me when I came here, that it is something like that. I have time to go to theatre, even if it cost very much, I didn't bother that it cost. It wasn't—it wasn't a problem, money. I wanted to go, I went. I want to go see friends, doesn't matter what it takes, day or half a day, it—in here, I think, oh, wow, I go see some people and—and half a day is gone, and that is this much, and much of money and people in my country can't earn very much money, so they don't—don't think about it too much. And they think it is—it is great. They can—I don't know if money is the most important value. . . .

[She was asked about special sounds in the Polish language.] And in Poland is very many of *sh—tch—sss,* this kind of sound. (*So you—*) Like very, ah, well, difficult to pronounce for very many people which try to learn Polish. _____ (*Oh, goodness, yes!*) It is "bug."

Title #9: Only a small amount of the original dialogue is excerpted for inclusion here. The speaker is saying that in 1934 his father bought a farm in eastern Poland, in the area that was taken over by the Russians at the

---

[2] "Zed" is a British pronunciation.

beginning of World War II and then was devastated by the later German advance toward Moscow.

Polish Family

I born in 1932. After '34, father buy farm, political for Russian, you know—after

terrible fighting, 1939, ya, you have to be Russian coming for Poland.

After _____ go the Russian for country. After they—I stay here six years,

Russian. (*You were in Russia six years?*) Ya. (*Were you fighting in Russia?*)

No—no, I was small boy. Only brother, we both, brother, you know, after they are

finish fighting, 1945, I have come into Poland. I stay here a couple of years after

coming to Canada in 1940—1964. . . .

(*Would you tell me about your family?*) Oh, my family is mother, two sister dead

for Russia. Ah, father, fif—1967 is dead. I got only one, only one family, sister and

brother, and stepmother for Poland. (*And you and your wife live here?*) Ya, here.

(*Children?*) Ya, two, two children—one girl, one boy. Is girl, girl married last year.

A boy not stay home, go to school.

LITHUANIA

Title #10: The speaker of the next title, a Lithuanian forester who is now living in the United States, is interviewed by his son, an American actor. The first few lines, used only because of the full-bodied sounds contained in them, are read from a script. The short body of dialogue that follows describes an experience that the father had when he performed in a play. The pauses, of course, are the result of a search for words.

A Nervous Face

First I will pronounce for you some separate words. I will say the word and then

I will pause so that you may repeat it after me. And then, in order that you may check yourself, I will say it again before I go to the next word. Here are the words.

. . .

(*You told me once that you used to do some acting.*) Yeah, sure. I was young. About 22 years—yeah, I, ah, acting this in Polish, one general, 1840—*nyet*—1831, in, in battle was Grochova. I, I was General Hoapitski. (*And were you, were you good?*) Yeah, I say, all people say I very good play. (*Were you nervous?*) Yeah, was, my all face nervous feel I have. (*Oh, your face shook?*) Shook. (*Trembled—*) Yeah. (*You were so nervous?*) Yes, I nervous. When I see whole people see me, maybe my colleague in all from navy, I have much trouble in self.

Asia

❧❧❧❧❧❧❧❧❧❧❧❧❧❧❧❧❧❧❧❧❧❧❧

China, Vietnam, India

CHINA

China and Japan are the two dominant nations in Asia. In early history both were sufficient unto themselves; intruders were not welcome. Later, both were opened up (in the Western sense), but only by force. The meaning in this for us is that there was a resistance by both countries to any penetration of the native language by outside elements. In the spoken form, the result shows in a marked difficulty to adapt the movements of the articulators—the lips, tongue, jaw, and, in some cases, the muscles of the throat—to the requirements of new syllabic formations. This means that certain English-language sounds are difficult to make—a fact that gives the accents a unique distinction. For example, the Chinese, like many other people around the world, have no equivalent of our *th*, voiced [ð] or voiceless [θ]. This means that the easier [d] or [z] usually is substituted, as it is also in Germany or France. Indeed, some Chinese officers in World War II, when they were asked to practice forming the *th*, not only resisted but were embarrassed by an action that caused the tongue to be extended forward far enough for it to rest against and slightly between the front teeth. In one group several of them snickered, as young boys used to do when they heard a forbidden word.

With regard to the Japanese accent, since for the last several decades relations between the United States and Japan have been close, the Japanese dialect was presented in depth in the first book, *Stage Dialects*.

It is only recently that any kind of relationship has existed between us and China, and presently it is a very limited one. However, there is no question that the Chinese, because of their size in territory and population and their new leadership, will be a major factor in world affairs; their influence beyond their own borders will be considerable. There is no doubt that the Chinese themselves think so, even though in recent times their Great Wall seems to have been a factual as well as a figurative symbol. Their very name for themselves indicates this: China, "The Middle Kingdom" (for "Middle" read "Center"), meaning that the Chinese have always regarded themselves and their concerns as being at the center of the world's affairs. Be that as it may, their contributions to

113

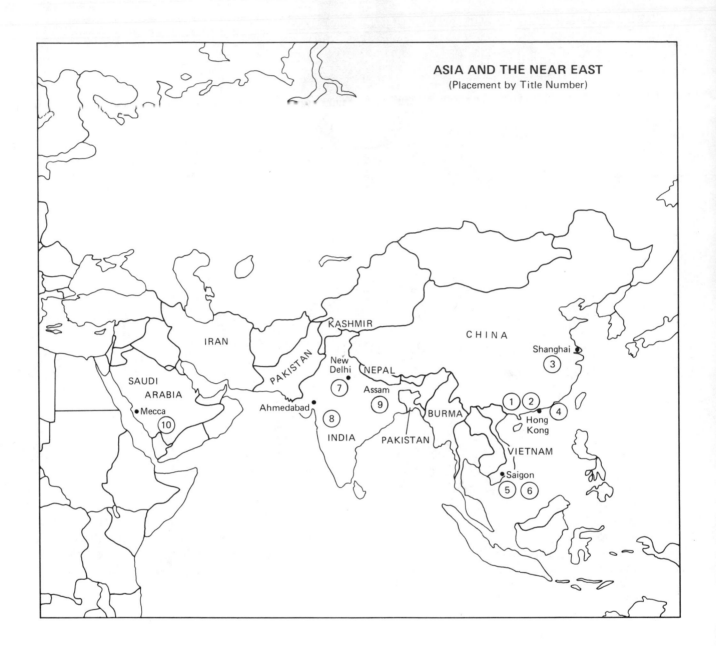

ASIA AND THE NEAR EAST
(Placement by Title Number)

world culture in philosophy, art, religion, medicine, and so on, are truly significant.

A Chinese accent is interesting, challenging, and distinctive. Here are the influences that bear upon it:

1. The language is monosyllabic; this means one word, one sound, the result of which is a short, clipped, and sometimes explosive series of sounds in a phrase or sentence. Sometimes, too, this is the cause of the rapidity with which it is spoken. These small explosions come after muscular stoppages, mostly in the pharynx, and they are similar to the glottal stop [ʔ] of the Cockney or the Scot; they will be marked with that symbol.

2. There are no tenses in the Chinese language; time is told quite simply by saying, "I go yesterday" or "I go tomorrow."

3. There are no articles, therefore, substantive words often stand by themselves.

4. A major element of expressiveness in the Chinese spoken language is the use of tones, that is, pitch inflections. A word uttered with one tone means one thing; the same word spoken with a different tone means something else. In the Mandarin dialect (the educated, political speech of Northern China) there are four tones: steady ——, short rise ⟋, quick fall and longer rise ⟍⟋, and fall ⟍. Southern Chinese or Cantonese speech has nine tones. These distinct pitch inflections cause what seems to Western ears a sing-song effect, but in the Chinese language they allow extra precision and expressiveness. However, this element does not play a major part in the accents that will be heard on the following tapes. What it does cause is a failure on the part of the articulators (lips, tongue, and jaw) to complete the necessary syllabic formations required of our words. The result is a slurred effect of words and phrases that are only partially pronounced: listen to *work*, *here*, *more*, and *Hong Kong-side* in the very beginning of the second tape.

5. In connection with the above, it should be noted that the lips are the least active of the articulators, as will be heard on the tapes. However, if an actor were to exploit this facet of the accent, a serious loss of clarity could result.

6. The most recognizable of the key sounds in this accent is the *r-l* problem. In simple but not quite correct terms, it could be said that *r* becomes *l* and *l* becomes *r*. When such an exchange does take place, as it does in the first title, "From Becomes Flom," the effect is immediately apparent. Most of the time, however, neither the *r* nor the *l* is fully formed, and each takes on something of the character of the other. Further, a terminal *l* or *ll* is often sounded as [lr], in which an [l] is begun but changed to a partial [r] before it is completely formed, as in Cockney speech and Vietnamese.

A second key sound to be noted is the familiar [i] for [ɪ], which alters *it* to *eat*.

7. Further, it will be seen that in most of the transcripts, the English vocabulary is severely limited, and the speakers use the fewest number of words possible to project their thoughts.

Title #1, Canton: The following short selection illustrates the full substitution of the *l* for the *r*, and it was included just for this reason.

From Becomes *Flom*

[*Where were you born in China?*] Canton (*Did you live there very long?*) Yes.

(*How long?*) Until my—go to the high school there. I over the north part of China,

Peking. (*And from Peking you came to America?*) No, from Peking I back to

Canton, Hong Kong, and from Hong Kong go to Taiwan, and from Taiwan go to

here.

Title #2, Hong Kong: Both the following transcript and Title #3 were taped in tailor shops during working hours, hence, the background sounds.

First Tailor

. . . I work here more about five year already, and I born in Hong Kong. I live in Kow—, Hong Kong side. Ya. (*Go to school?*) Ah, yeah, we go to school. (*Ah, where?*) In Hong Kong side. (*How long you go to school?*) Oh, about ten year. (*Ten year. What did you study?*) Oh, we study all kind of subject, you see—arithmetic, you know, geography, history, all different kind, you see. We had not only one subject, we had not study only one, we study all the subject. (*Then what is your present position?*) Present position, ah—ah, I passed the, the certificate of origin[1]—the certificate of the Hong Kong government. (*The—the what?*) I mean we pass the middle school. (*Middle school.*)

(*Now what do you do here?*) I work here as a salesman. (*You're a salesman? How long have you worked here?*) Oh, more than five year. (*What all do you sell?*) Oh, all the different kind—silk, brocade, and woolen, any kind, you see, and we do very nice men's and ladies' tailor here. (*You think this is a good shop?*) Oh, yeah, this is the best shop in Hong Kong. Yeah! Yeah! (*You have to say that because you work here.*) Yeah, that's right, and we know that we're the—the high reputation in Hong Kong, too! You, you try our tailoring, you know that, you see—

Title #3, Shanghai: The second tailor speaks at a more deliberate pace.

[1] He confused his certification of graduation from high school with the "Certificate of Origin," which must accompany all goods bought in Hong Kong to signify to U.S. customs that the articles were not on the list of forbidden goods from Mainland China.

Second Tailor

. . . (*How long have you been here?*) I will been here about 15 years already.

(*Were you born in Hong Kong?*) No, we from Shanghai. (*How long?*) About 15

years ago. (*Fifteen years ago. Why did you leave Shanghai?*) Shanghai because

now is a Communist state, see, and nobody make the new clothes. (*Ah.*)

Everybody come to Hong Kong. (*So for tailors, Shanghai is not good.*) Shanghai

tailor is best of tailor in the world. (*Yes, but nobody buys suit.*) But nobody buy

suit, only the cotton suit. (*Ah—huh.*) We expect better for men's tailor. (*Now, did

you come with your family?*) No. (*Then your family is—*) In Shanghai still. (*Is still in

Shanghai. Can you go see them?*) No—no—is very hard go over there . . . there'd

be somethings trouble.

Title #4, Hong Kong: The following selection, which was taped in a
speech laboratory, offers the listener an exceptionally good model of a
strong, distinctive, and clear accent.

A New American

[*Do you like living in Los Angeles?*] Yeah, I like Los Angeles very good. I like it,

the school, the education, the—it's a, the education's a free from first grade to high

school. I don't have to pay anything. No, I learn the typing, piano, guitar. . . . but

in Hong Kong from first grade to high school, they have to pay a lot of money for

the books, I mean, for the stationery.

   (*Did you like your life in Hong Kong?*) Well, not too, not really, because a too

crowd, and . . . (*Do you like sports?*) Ya, I like sports. (*What sports?*) Bowling,

that's my favorite sport, and I like to ride a car, too. (*Tell me about bowling.*)

Bowling? (*Are you good at bowling?*) No, my average is not too good, only—sometime a 80, sometimes a 100, yeah. (*Why do you like bowling?*)

Because a—I enjoy it when my ball roll all the way down and then the ball all the

way tell down, something like that. (*Knock all the pins down?*) Yeah, knock all pin

down—(*Un-huh*)—ten pin down. (*Un-huh*) I like that, and I like the noise, just like a

thunder. . . .

VIETNAM

Each of the nations of Southeast Asia—Vietnam, Laos, Thailand, Cambodia, and Malaysia—has a language of its own. Yet when a native of any one of them speaks in English, the accent is similar to that of all the others.[2] Accordingly, for the purposes of our study, Vietnam is an excellent representative of the whole group. Two donors from Vietnam present us with interesting transcripts.

The several characteristics that mark this strong and distinguished accent are the following:

1. A dropping of final consonants is often heard. In the first transcript listen to the words *small*, *boat*, *want*, and *because*.

2. The [lr] syndrome, which will be heard again and again (as in Chinese and Japanese), is prevalent. This particular phoneme is explained in Chapter III of *Stage Dialects:*

[2] It should be noted that in each of these nations, indeed throughout the whole larger area of Southest Asia, Chinese nationals and emigrees, even those of several generations back, maintain with remarkable stability and endurance their native speech and customs, sometimes to the point of causing enmity and even hostility in the local population. An ability to prosper is one of their characteristics.

[lr] is a designation of [r] substituted for medial or terminal [l]. [r] is substituted for a medial or terminal [l] (*l* or *ll*) in a manner previously heard only in lower middle-class English or Cockney speech. The unique feature of this exchange is that the crossover is not complete, neither a full [l] nor a full [r] is sounded. The [r] predominates, however, it being the last sound formed. To achieve the proper effect, begin to make an [l], with the tip of the tongue extended toward the alveolar or upper gum ridge. Then, while the tip is extended but before it touches the ridge, form and enunciate an [r]. The resultant mixture of these two consonants produces the desired effect. . . . Since there is no phonetic designation for this sound, we will adapt [lr] to the purpose. . . .

3. The influence of the French language (for a long period France was the dominant colonial power in this area) can be heard in the [i] (*eat*) for [ɪ] (*it*) substitution, as well as in a [d] or [z] replacement of *th* [ð], very softly here.

4. There is a tendency to alter the established vowel in a variety of words, for example, *yes* and *place*. Since this is done on a random basis, it indicates unfamiliarity more than anything else.

Both Vietnamese donors were taped in only partially quiet circumstances, hence, the background sounds heard on the tapes.

Title #5: The following donor, a young lady just out of her teens, after the death of her father and mother was responsible for her smaller brothers and sisters as they made their escape from Saigon and the incoming Communist troops.

Escape

(*Would you tell me again about how you left Saigon and got to Thailand?*) Yes.

When the Communists took over my country that day, ah, May, '75, and I was afraid they cotch, cotch us and we decided to run away and then we went to Gacong,

the, ah, that place, my auntie, he live there. Then my auntie bought a, give us a

small boat then we, we went to the sea. The first day in the small boat some, some

soldiers kill—hit, hit, and kill together, because they want to kill us—I know, I know

exactly that reason. Because they thought that we are, we—we were rich people.

And they, they ki—they destroyed all machine in, in that boat, and that boat trip

very dangerous. I, I thought that we, we had, we had died, but the God that love us

gave us to live.

(*Did you have any food?*) We, we had, we had a little food, and I have a small

bottle of water and, I were sitting on, on small bottle of water because I'm afraid

the soldier, ah, if they saw it, they will took it because the machine, the machine

need water. And they will put water in the machine and we have no water and we

will die.

(*How long were you on the sea?*) I have about five ni—, five days and six nights

on the sea. (*After that long time on the sea, where did you finally land?*) We land in

Thailand. (*Were you happy to get there?*) Yes, and we happy! (*Very happy?*) Yes.

Title #6: The donor of the following selection, working in a sponsorship
program, is continuing his education here in the United States.

Naval Officer

. . . (*And where do you come from?*) I was born in South Vietnam, and growing

up, ah, about 17 years, until—17 years old, I, ah, go to school. And I graduate from

high school when I was 18 old year. At that time I want to be officer in the navy, so

I register in the navy college. Ah, after 2 year for study, and 1 year for practice in

the ocean, I become officer in the navy of my, of South Vietnam government.

(*Did you have a very active career during the war, or was it fairly quiet?*) Ah, in

the ocean it was not much fight over there. Most of the fight is in the mountain. But,

an, sometimes I, I have some, some relationship become my life and the war—like

when I take vacation and the war is over in my place so, but is terrible

in _____ because I saw lot people die, and blood and something like that.

(*How did you get out of Saigon, Vietnam?*) Umm at, at that time I was working in

the ocean, Pacific Ocean and, ah, the radio it said the government, the South

Vietnam government is fell down, and I think is no place to go so I try to row to

Thailand or Philippine, and after I drive the ship about three hour, or four hour so

the United States navy communication with us, and they tell with us follow with

them to Subic Bay.

INDIA

For years, when the huge subcontinent of India was a part of the British Empire, if any native spoke English, either well or poorly, it was in the accents of the quasi-official language of the official ruling class, and that language was Standard English. Those who spoke it well could sound as British as any Briton. Others, less proficient, spoke a Standard English that was altered by the accents of their native tongue. This lingual situation existed for all the time of British rule. The clipped precision of the speech sounded like that of an official pronouncement or even like the chatter that might be heard outside a West-end theatre during intermission; the sounds stressed the broad *a*'s and rounded and hollowed *o*'s, all flowing up and down the vocal scale with that remarkable British range.

However, with the coming of independence, old language ties were broken, giving new lingual influences a chance to exert themselves. The result is an Indian accent that falls into three categories:

1. The Standard English speech of an older generation, or of those educated in England. Although this influence is losing its force, there are large numbers of Indians who still unite the exactness of

Standard English with their own vocal characteristics in what is often a very attractive blend.

2. The large body of Indians who have learned English (it is compulsory in most schools) from Indian teachers. This group (you will hear two of them) has a delivery that is shaped much more by the key sounds and the tempo and melodic patterns of their native tongue than by the sounds of ''proper'' English.

3. Those Indians who have emigrated (there are large numbers of them) and are learning English in the accents of the countries to which they have come, for example, the United States, Canada, and the Caribbean.

As for the Indian accent itself, two major characteristics immediately assert themselves. The first of these is the rapid rate of delivery. While speech tempo usually is a personal characteristic no matter what the language is, in this case it is a national trait. The second of these is a remarkable flexibility of lips, tongue, and jaw, which gives the speech a precision that is unusual in most accents.

Two other tendencies used to be as pronounced as those listed above but are now fast dying out. One is a higher than usual pitch level for all sounds, which is caused, probably, by smaller than usual vocal chords located in smaller than usual bodies. The other is a melodic inflection much like the pitch patterns of the Welsh. Although it is heard infrequently today, both of these tendencies are attractive and usable.

The key sounds to be noted vary somewhat among the three transcripts in this series. Of them all, a single tapped or a slightly trilled *r* is the most common. There is also a very soft *d* that will be used in place of the voiced *th* [ð], as in *the*, making [də]. Then a *v* will replace a *w*, and once in a while a *k* will be added to *ing*. There are also vowel and diphthong changes that are too subtle to be given a different phonetic symbol but that will be heard nonetheless.

Title #7, New Delhi: The donor in the following transcript is a well-known Indian dancer who was good enough to take time to talk about things other than dance. His manner of delivery is the most distinctive element in the piece. The key sound changes are not many and are often quite subtle. For this reason, the phonetic markings will appear in the second title rather than in the first one.

Several single items might be noted: the extra [ə] that is added to so many words; the eliding of others, as in *Taj Mahal;* and an acceleration in the rate of speaking beyond the norm, heard in the first tape.

The Taj Mahal

[*Would you tell me something about the famous Taj Mahal?*] Taj Mahal is located, is about a couple—a couple of hundred miles away from New Delhi. And Taj Mahal is built by Emperor Shah Jahan in the memory of his beloved wife, Muntaz Mahal. And the, no, emperor was very much in love with the queen, and the queen asked him once that, "How you will remember my love?" The emperor told her that, "I am going to build such a big building, of such a big monument of love, it is going to be a source of inspiration for the coming time."

So 22, 20, about 22 years continuously and the—the laborers were working on that monument, and they changed the whole all-white marble is changed into a pure and beautiful piece of love. . . .

(*Would you tell me something about Kashmir?*) Kashmir—when you talk about Kashmir, it give me a sort of sensation. I have a chance to visit Kashmir when I—when I was in my college. We went to Kashmir, and it's my feeling that Kashmir is the Switzerland of India. (*It is what?*) Is the Switzerland of India, as Switzerland is very much famous in the world, and the same is—when I recollect that I was

staying in a boat, in a houseboat, you know, when I'm talking to you it all, I am

reflecting the whole that ever happen about 7 years back. It's just like heaven on

the earth, you know. You can ski—you can go for skiing there. You can go the

houseboats, houseboats are style like Western—like Western hotel, as well as

Indian style. And you feel that you have come to a place which you can imagine,

and imagine, and that is Kashmir.

Title #8, Ahmedabad: The donor of the next selection is just beginning her study of English, so the reader should be tolerant of her struggling. However, she gives us excellent primary source material to work on. The transcript was taped in a speech laboratory in Los Angeles. In addition to the key sounds listed at the beginning of this series, you will note that she consistently substitutes the [i], as in *eat,* for the [ɪ], as in *it.* Vocabulary and word order are obvious problems. Special attention should be given to her practice of placing emphasis on the final syllable of many words, which is a characteristic of much Indian speech: note *city, India, country, husband, baby, English,* and so forth.

For *Too Much* translate *Very Good* or *Very Much.*

Too Much

. . . I came from Inꞌdia. (*How long have you been here?*) I have been here, ah,

about three years. (*And where was your home in India?*) Ahmedabad ciꞌty.

(*Do you like this country?*) Ya! I like this counꞌtry. My husband, ah, likes too

much this counꞌtry. Ah, my baꞌby, ah, goes to nurꞌsery school now. (*What does

he do in nursery school?*) Ah, just for play, and something, loves, ah, his nurꞌsery

school. He speaks—he speaks too much in Engꞌlish and our language, Gujaratli.

He's a very naughꞌty boy—"Mummy, tell me stoꞌry in Engꞌlish," ah, he say me.

Ah, he likes too much stoꞌry, ah, he asks in our language and in Engꞌlish

language stoꞌry, both.

(*What stories do you tell him?*) Ah, in India, ah, my law father [father-in-law] send us, ah, some magazines—(*And you read stories from—*) Ya, I read stories every day, bed time, my son hear. (*And do you read him stories in English, too?*) Ya, in English do I read. He understand all. I don't tell in my language, just I read. (*Oh, yes.*) Ya, he speaks too much.

(*And what do you like about this country?*) Ah, I like Los Angeles. I don't see many things here. (*You have not traveled?*) Griffith Park—Griffith Park, Lion Country Safari I go—(*And what did you see in the Lion Safari?*) Ya, Lion Country Safari, we sat in the car, ah, closed car, and we saw, ah, too much lion together, and, ah, all—all animals, ah, just like giraffe, and elephants too much together, and, ah, zebra. (*Did you have any elephants in your part of India?*) Ya, ah, in the zoo. . . .

[A question was asked about India's great leader, Nehru.] Jawaharlal Nehru, he was a Prime Minister in India. (*Was he a great man?*) Ya, great man. He's a great man. (*Why was he a great man?*) Ah, his nature is very good, he likes children too much, small children. He plays, ah, little children. His nature is that type.

Title #9, Assam: If the following speaker had been taped 25 years ago, beyond question her speech would have been Standard English against a background of her native tongue; now only traces of that once established speech remain. What is apparent is a remarkable flexibility, which gives a clarity to her speech in spite of the rapid pace. Both of these traits are of use in developing this accent. Vocabulary and sentence construction are well above average, but it is not unusual among the educated of this new nation. The clipped speech, however, is the title's most distinctive feature and the principal reason for its inclusion.

Indian Student

. . . I was in a totally girls' college, and we had little hostels about—of about hundred girls, and the college has about 2,000—between 2,500 and 2,000 students. And it's full girls in that college, no boys. But it comes under the

Rajastan University, and the university has different colleges. Our college was

called Maharani College, and right across the road there was a college called

Maharaja College, and that has boys. (*Well, that was very convenient then, wasn't

it?*) Yes, in some cases, yes. [There was further dialogue, then—]

(*Would you tell me something about your acting?*) Well, ah—(*What plays were

you in?*) Once I took part in an English play, and once in a Hindi play—Hindi is our

national language. And in the English one I didn't have much of a part, but in the

Hindi one, yes, I had—(*What was the English play?*) The English play was about

an old couple who are sitting in their house, and they don't realize that actually

there's a director who comes into the room and they don't see him. They are too

old. And he—and they start enacting a play in the room, you know, about—it's a

crook coming in and the heroine shouting and things. And these two people are

just wondering what's going on. And they get very scared, and they start shouting.

It's a comedy. So I was—I was supposed to be the heroine of the—of the play in

the play. And of course I was yelling away and screaming away and running to the

guy, you know, and clinging on to him. And there's the crook, and there's the gun,

and things like that.

The Near East

ᘓᘏᘓᘏᘓᘏᘓᘏᘓᘏᘓᘏᘓᘏᘓᘏᘓᘏᘓᘏᘓᘏᘓᘏᘓᘏᘓᘏᘓᘏ

SAUDI ARABIA

Title #10, The speaker of the following selection, a fine-arts major from Mecca, was taped in Los Angeles in a speech laboratory between a session on English pronunciation and one on grammar. Like so many foreign students in this country, he was eager for more contact with Americans, so that he might enjoy the give-and-take of ordinary conversation, but strangely enough, not many were willing to give the time for such an exchange. This denial might make for a good dialect or accent, but it is scarcely beneficial to the visitor.

As is usual with most accents, a few key sounds immediately catch our attention: in this case, it is first the *r*, tapped or slightly trilled; second, the substitution, on an inconsistent basis, of *b* for *p*, as when *pray* becomes *bray* (there is no *p* in Arabic). There is also the tendency, in a two-syllable word, to give equal emphasis to both syllables. You will hear this in *Mecca, student, only, garden, Moslem,* and so on. The limited vocabulary and confused word order will be apparent. Not consistent and not strong are a few other substitutions: *z* for *th* [ð], as in *the; f* for *v*, as in *every;* a terminal *t* for *d*, as in *God;* and a *k* ending for *ing*, as in *painting.*

The Painter from Mecca

    r^r   ao r^r   r^r
I am from Saudi Arabia. I am from Mec'ca. I was born in Mec'ca, and I was stu,dent

   ao r^r   z
in Saudi Arabia. I finish my, ah, elementary school, and I went to the [in]stitute

because I will be a tea'cher, and I want to be a tea'cher, and I work as tea'cher

over there about 16 years, and then my government send me to United States to

study in my subject. (*And what is your subject?*) My subject is fine art,

painting. . . .

[A question was asked about what subjects can be painted by a Moslem.]

. . . but we didn't paint people. We paint only any subject like mountains, or

garden. I can't explain by English this reason. Is hard reason because like if, ah,

when Islam come the people would pray for the people,[1] not for the God.

Every—every group of people has God, and this God, like statue—statue? (*Ah,*

statue!) Statue (*yes*), statue or picture of somebody, and they pray for this picture

and they call this statue our God.

So when Islam—Islam came, broke all the statue, and say nobody make picture

for anybody because if he make this picture, he going to like this picture, and love

this picture, and then he going to pray for this picture, and he going to say this

picture is our God. So Islam says, no, that is no picture. When you can draw

mountains, flowers, trees, everything in the—all you can— . . .

[*Would you tell me something about the city of Mecca?*] Mecca is the city of the

rel—religion, religions. Ah, every years the Mos—Islamic people come to Mecca

for pilgrim. They come every year, and there, in Mecca, there is a holy Kaaba, you

know, the Kaaba is a—we call House of—the House of God. (*The House of God.*)

The House of God, the Kaaba. And they come to Kaaba, and then go to another

place in Mecca for—for pilgrim. Every Muslim have to do this one time in his life,

one time.

[1] The reference here is to the worship of graven images, as in the Bible.

(*Are there any other holy cities?*) Ah, there is Medina, is Medina. Medina, there is a mosque of the Prophet Mohammed in Medina, and he was died there in Medina, Prophet Mohammed. So the whole Muslim, Moslem when they will to Mecca—they have to go to Medina also to visit the mosque of Prophet Mohammed.

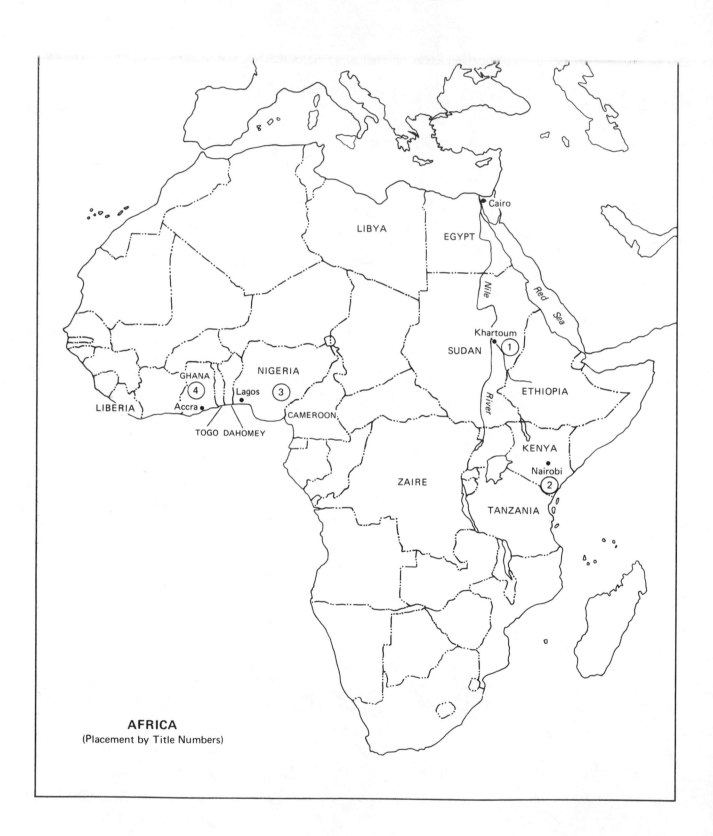

AFRICA
(Placement by Title Numbers)

Africa

Sudan, Kenya, Nigeria, Ghana

The accents selected for representation here are those of Black Africa, representing the North Central area, as well as the East Coast and the West Coast. The portion of Africa that borders on the Mediterranean is, in most cases, an extension of Europe and for this reason is not included here. Similarly, the southernmost area, which is under the domination of South Africa, also is not covered.

In the broad sweep of Middle or Equatorial Africa, which is where our representation concentrates, there are many different native or tribal languages. Nearly all of these at one time or another have been acted upon by outside influences. In the North Central and East Coast areas, Arabic and perhaps Indian vocal patterns have been present for at least 1,200 years. In those same areas, as well as in the Middle and West Coast portions of the continent, European influences from conquering and colonizing agents also have been present for at least 90 to 100 years. Of these, English, French (Belgian), and Portuguese were and are the most

influential, with English (England being the dominal colonial power) obviously the principal lingual influence.

From the beginning, one thing should be understood about the accent of an African speaking English today. Untutored speech is a disappearing phenomenon and is heard only in remote villages or the bush, and Tarzan-like utterances are an absurdity. The language of the continent, of towns and cities, of commerce, government, education, and international relations demonstrate a high degree of lingual skills in which Africans not only speak their own tongue but are likely to be adept in one or several other languages as well, for example, Arabic, English, and French, their expressiveness matching that of persons who have multilingual abilities. Further, like any other non English-speaking individuals, their speech in the English language reflects the pronunciations of their native tongue. Outside of this, as the tapes will show, fluency and expressiveness are to be expected.

SUDAN

Title #1: The early history of Sudan is the history of Ancient Egypt, of which it was a part as far back as the time of the Old Kingdom, 3400 to 2100 B.C. In the eight century, A.D., an Arabic invasion established an Islamic presence that in language and culture still exists in strength today; the invaders gave a name to the country, Bilad-as-Sudan, "The Country of the Blacks." Then, in the last part of the nineteenth century, when the British conquered and colonized the area, English was established as the official language, and it was taught in the schools and used in all military and governmental activities. Thus, three lingual cultures are present and can be heard whenever English is used as a communicative tool in the independent country of Sudan today: Egyptian, Arabic, and British.

The donor of the following title, a well-informed and helpful individual, was an official of the present Sudanese mission to the United Nations; he was willing to sacrifice attending a session at the United Nations to provide this tape. An air conditioner hums in the background.

The major characteristics of the Sudanese accent are:

1. The precise articulation or syllabic clip, which is indigenous to so much of the speech of the Near East and Africa. This important feature can and should be used to advantage whenever possible.
2. The separated or guttural [ȟ] of the Arabic, for example, *Khartoum.*
3. A trilled or a tapped *r* [rʳ], which is not always consistently employed.
4. An [s] for the *th* [θ], as in *north, south, with,* and so on.
5. A [d] or a [z] for the voiced *th* [ð].
6. The Arabic substitution of [b] for [p], there being no *p* in that language, for example, *independent.*
7. An [s] for a [z], for example, [wɑs] for [wɑz].
8. An unusual pronunciation in which the [ɛʳ] of *air* replaces the [ɜʳ] of *her,* so that *her* sounds like *hair* to which a tongue tap has been added, for example, *first, third,* and *university.* (This pronunciation is much in use in a Scots dialect and in Greek and Romanian accents as well.)
9. An [f] for a [v], as heard in *province.*

(A sibilant *s* needs monitoring in this transcript.)

Information Officer

. . . I waṡ born in Omdurman and, you know, Omdurman, ah, is a major city in the province of Khartoum. The province of Khartoum is composed of three major cities, that's to say, Khartoum, which is the capital of Sudan, Khartoum-North, and

Omdurman. (*We call it Khartoum. Is it Khartoum?*) Is ȟ—Kȟartoum. You know, in

Arabic you, to pronounce ȟ—Kȟartoum, but you spell it Khartoum. (*And that is the*

north or south part of the country?) It's in the center of Sudan, where the Blue

Nile join the White Nile and then they compose the Nile which goes to the north.

[*What is the main occupation of the country?*] Agriculture. (*Yes.*) And you know

by the way, Sudan, ah, according to the United Nation, is supposed to be, ah, one

of three countries who are going to contribute towards the solution of all food crisis

which the world is expected to face in the 25 years to come. (*Oh, yes.*) So Sudan is

mainly an agricultural country.

[*In your educational system, when do the children start to school?*] Well, they

start about 4 or 5, when the child is 4 or 5 years then he goes to what we call

Rowda, to prepare the student before he joins the school. When the child is 7

years then he starts his proper education and he joins the elementary school. And

the first year he studies general mathematics, Arabic language, and religion. If he

is a Moslem, that's if he is from the north, he studies Islam, Islam religion. If he is

Christian, then he will study Christianity.

[There was a question about the history of Sudan.] Yeah, we, you know, the

history of Sudan is one that traces back, you have to go to the very long time ago.

You know, in Sudan there were independent kingdoms in Sudan and at

about _____ time even there was something like an empire, and at

about _____ stage of its history Sudan has even colonized Egypt for a very

long time.

KENYA

Title #2: The accommodating young Kenyan in the next transcript is a
representative of his government here in the United States; he is

representative also of the spoken English of his country. As a member of one of the several native language groups of Kenya, his pronunciation of the key sounds of Kenyan English is identical with those of the members of the country's other tribal groups. He was taped in the office of the Kenyan Consulate in Beverly Hills, California, hence the voices heard in the background.

You will hear the following key sounds on the tape: *a*, especially marked in *and* [ɑndə], with the unemphasized schwa vowel [ə] tacked on; the *r*, tapped [rʳ] and dropped [ɾ]; a *d* for *th* [ð]; an occasional [i], as in *eat*, for [ɪ], as in *it;* the secondary accent which is heard in such words as *Africa*, *eastern*, and *equator*.

The rapidity of the donor's delivery will attract your attention, which is a characteristic that the good actor will suggest rather than reproduce. In this respect, the slurring of terminal syllables can be a problem. In a different case, it will be noted that the exactly right word does not always come to meet the speaker's need.

National Parks

(*Would you tell me where you are from?*) I'm from Kenya. (*And where in* [*is*] Kenya?) Well, to be exact, Kenya is in Afri ca, on the eas' tern Afri ca, and we have Equa' tor passing right through Kenya. And to be more specific about the coun' try, it's located—on our northern side we have Ethiopia, eastern we have Somalia, on the west we have Uganda, and south is Tanzania, and then the Indian coast [Ocean] is our—you know, on our coast.

. . . Well, Kenya is world-wide known for its, it's a home of wild life. Mention of any animal, mention it, we have so many animals. (*What are some of the famous national parks?*) We have Amboseli, we have Tsavo, we have Meru, many, you know, so many. (*Where does the tourist stay when he is there?*) We have so many lodges in national park. We have very, very beautiful hotels within the national parks. As a matter of—when you in the hotel you won't realize you are in, in the bush until you step out of your door to see the elephant there, to see the lion there, to see giraffe there.

I'll give you an incident that happened last, ah, about three months ago. (*Oh, yes.*) Oh, I was in, I went back to Kenya for a visit and, ah, I went to Amboseli National Park. I had gone there for the weekend, since it's a long time since I've been there. Okay, ah, when I woke up in the morning, I could see the sun was coming through the window and after stretching I said let me open the window for fresh air, and guess what was there? I couldn't open my window, the elephant was leaning next to my hut. (*What did you do?*) It was really amazing after, you know, when I've been here for a long time and every time I open the window it's a long time since I've experienced something like an elephant within the reach. I never think I [*can*] open the window because an elephant going to look through the other window. (*Did that elephant leave? Did he go away?*) I, I didn't get bothered at all, didn't get bothered at all. . . .

NIGERIA

Title #3: The following donor, a student majoring in industrial technology, has been in the United States for three years. He speaks of the troubled times of the Ibo people during the civil war in Nigeria some years back.

Civil War

(*How are conditions in your country now?*) Ah, well, presently things are not very favorable, I would say, no. But on the whole, it's better than it had been in the past few years in a, mostly since after we have had a, some revolution in the country some several disturbance in the country. And currently we have a military government in the country, but I would say things are much better than they were three years ago.

(*How were conditions earlier, during the time of the, the major revolution?*) Ah, well, it was a very troubled time, you know, to speak of, it was very trouble. Many

people died of hunger and a, naturally was a very intense war in which many

people died, you know, were fighting throughout the three years of the, of the

fighting period there was no cease-fire until the last day. (*No cease-fire?*) Yeah,

there was no cease-fire, and many fronts opened every day and a, each, each

fighting resulted in new casualties, and there were no places to house our

wounded soldiers, and civilians died of hunger and soldiers likewise.

(*Were you involved, personally, in the war?*) Yes, I was involved. As long as

any, any, any person then in the a, in the eastern Nigerian, in eastern Nigeria who

were of the age of 11, now was involved in the war. (*How were you involved? Did*

you fight?) Yes, I had—yes, I fought. Yeah, I remember I was in high school and

after I left school I joined the Fire Service, and from Fire Service I joined Boys'

Company. . . . In the Boys' Company is a, it is some form, you know, it is some

form of a fighting warfare tactics [guerrilla] in which young people, children, were

used. They would disguise, you know, and pretend they were wounded or, or they

were abandoned by their parents, and they would go into the fighting zone and be

picked up by the others' soldiers on the other part who would, who would try to,

you know, try to comfort them, and later on they would escape, and (*and bring*

information back?) and bring information back, yes. Many children died as a result

of that, too.

GHANA

Title #4: The two short excerpts in the next title are included for the
specific purpose of showing the influence of our own American speech on
that of a person from a foreign-language group. The speaker, a native of
Ghana, had previously spent some time in Europe before coming to this
country. He has been here now for several years, long enough for him to

have acquired, for good or otherwise, some of our distinctive key sounds, as well as several of our colloquial expressions. The change of the voiced *th* [ð] to *d,* a practice of non-English-speaking persons all over the world, will be heard immediately.

Civil Engineer

I'm from Ghana, yeah, you know—that's right. I'm, you know, I'm going back as an engineer and as a manager at the same time, to, you know, I'll put it this way, that, you know, this engineering management, you know, which is one of the badly needed areas in Africa right now. (*Now what kind of engineering will you specialize in?*) That's in civil engineering. That's a, yeah, like road building, you know, road construction, yeah, and also general structural, you know, buildings, and things like that, you know. . . .

[His children had previously visited his home village in Ghana.] (*When the kids went back—*) Yeah, when my kids went back, right, and they were playing with their friends, you know, their new friends they made there, right? They spoke English, right, and their friends didn't understand English. But, ah, my big son, you know, he wouldn't explain anything. Oh, he could have, I know, but he wouldn't do it. But the middle one, you know, would take his time and try to explain games or, you know, how to run a play and things like that, you know, yeah.

Subject Index

Title Index

80 81 82 9 8 7 6 5 4 3 2 1